WHERE TO WILDLIFE

in Berkshire, Buckinghamshire & Oxfordshire

Edited by Sue Mitchell and Geoffrey Young

First published 1989
Second edition 1991
Third edition 1994
Fourth edition 1996

British Library-in-Publication Data.
A catalogue record for this book is available from the British Library.

ISBN 1-874357-11-0

Designed and published for BBONT by the Nature Conservation Bureau Ltd, Newbury
Printed by Information Press, Oxford

BBONT is part of a nationwide network of Local Trusts which work to protect wildlife in town and country.
 Through their care of 2,000 nature reserves the Wildlife Trusts are dedicated to the achievement of a UK richer in wildlife, managed on sustainable principles.
 Sharing this goal and making a vital contribution to its attainment are the junior wing Wildlife WATCH and the Urban Wildlife Groups around the country.
 Using their specialist skills in the fields of conservation and education, The Wildlife Trusts strive to win public recognition that the achievement of their aims is essential for a healthy environment and continued human existence.

Contents

Acknowledgements

BBONT would like to thank the following people for their help with the production of this book:

Michael Horwood, who wrote the original BBONT Nature Reserves Handbook on which many of the reserve descriptions are based; Geoffrey Young who compiled the 1989 edition with help from others too numerous to mention; Pete Creed for his design work combined with his wildlife expertise and intimate knowledge of the nature reserves, which contributed greatly to the accuracy and detail in all editions; Wendy Cunningham for compiling this latest reprint with the help of conservation staff and volunteer reserve managers.

Foreword

Those of us who live within the counties of Berkshire, Buckinghamshire and Oxfordshire are very aware of the benefits and pleasures offered by our beautiful countryside. This great variety of landscape and wildlife is largely the result of human activities over many hundreds of years. However, in the last century or so the impact of this activity has become greatly damaging to our wildlife. Increased industrial and commercial development and more intensive agricultural processes have taken their toll and will continue to do so unless we all strive to correct the balance.

BBONT's nature reserves are central to its work for a better future for our wildlife. They provide protection for some of our very rare species of animals and plants as well as giving people the opportunity to enjoy and appreciate the rich variety of habitats which were once widespread. They are the 'jewels in the crown' – indeed more than half of BBONT's nature reserves are Sites of Special Scientific Interest.

By supporting your local Wildlife Trust, you will be helping to protect our wildlife for generations to come. This book provides a guide to BBONT's special wildlife places in the three counties. They are there for everyone to enjoy.

Martin Spray
Director of BBONT

What is BBONT?

The Berkshire, Buckinghamshire and Oxfordshire Naturalists' Trust (BBONT) is one of a national network of County Wildlife Trusts. BBONT represents its members who want to protect wildlife in the three counties. In the last few years, BBONT has saved: ★ 16 ancient woodlands; ★ 500 acres of prime downland; ★ 24 wetland sites and lakes; ★ 21 old flower meadows; ★ 125 acres of heathland.

BBONT is an independent registered charity and a member of 'The Wildlife Trusts', the national partnership of wildlife trusts, urban wildlife groups and Wildlife WATCH, the junior club.

What does BBONT do?

Many wildlife habitats have been and are continuing to be destroyed, so there is a need for organisations such as BBONT. Like the other County Trusts, BBONT is involved in protecting local wildlife habitats and in encouraging people to learn about and enjoy our unique wildlife heritage. BBONT works to protect wildlife in several ways:

★ BBONT looks after over 90 nature reserves in the three counties. These sites are often havens for rare or endangered species, many being Sites of Special Scientific Interest. Most BBONT nature reserves are open to the public.

★ BBONT seeks to influence the planning process, making sure that planning applications, road schemes etc. take wildlife into account.

★ BBONT gathers and holds information on wildlife which helps to better identify threats and losses and to take necessary action.

★ BBONT runs special projects, such as the Upper Thames Otter Habitat Project, which endeavour to improve habitats so that wildlife will return to them.

★ BBONT seeks to encourage farmers, local authorities, industry and all landowners to manage their land in a more wildlife-friendly way.

★ BBONT has a programme of illustrated talks, wildlife walks and nature reserve work parties which inform and involve the public in practical nature conservation. In addition, some larger nature reserves have interpretative signs to explain how nature reserves are managed, and wildlife walk leaflets to guide visitors around the reserves.

★ BBONT, as part of 'The Wildlife Trusts', has a junior club, Wildlife WATCH, for under-18s. Members receive a magazine, badges, competitions and the opportunity to take part in nationwide wildlife surveys. There are also many local WATCH groups, run by volunteers, which provide opportunities for young people to join in wildlife activities and conservation projects. The magazines and activities are particularly appropriate for children aged between 7 and 12.

★ BBONT raises money for its work through membership, fundraising, events, sponsorship, legacies, donations and grants. There is also a Wildlife Shop in Wallingford which sells wildlife-friendly products. The profits go directly to the work of the charity.

★ BBONT runs a consultancy which provides a service to companies, local authorities, landowners and others who require expert advice on wildlife issues. The work includes landscape plans, detailed ecological surveys, environmental impact assessments and advice on educational and recreational facilities.

Who does the work?

BBONT has several hundred volunteers. These volunteers are members of the general public who give their time to help look after nature reserves, run events, distribute newsletters, help with administration, lead guided walks and give wildlife talks. Their contribution, whether large or small, enables BBONT to carry out its work in the three counties.

In addition, BBONT has a small number of staff who are responsible for organising the many different areas of the wildlife trust's work, from conservation, membership and administration to publicity, fundraising and education.

Why do we need nature reserves?

In Britain today, the survival of wildlife often takes second place to human activity. Towns and road networks expand, woodlands make way for housing estates and rivers are polluted. Perhaps the most dramatic changes to our countryside have occurred because of developments in agriculture and forestry. Small fields, hedgerows and coppiced woodlands have in many cases been replaced by large fields with arable crops, sprayed with chemicals and cultivated by huge machines. These developments have occurred because of pressures on the farming community to increase food production, but the diversity of plants and animals in the countryside has been seriously reduced in the process. In an effort to look after what remains, we have had to create nature reserves. These are needed for several reasons:

★ They are wildlife havens in a countryside which can no longer support the rich wildlife which used to be widespread in our counties. BBONT nature reserves include broadleaved woods, chalk downland, marshes, hay meadows, bogs and heath, hedgerows and even disused railway lines and gravel pits.

★ They act as 'reservoirs' of species, from which wildlife could spread back into the countryside if conditions became favourable.

★ They are places for scientific study of wildlife.

★ They are places for the public to visit and enjoy, allowing people to appreciate and understand wildlife, and encouraging them to help protect it.

The countryside then ...

... and now.

Looking after nature reserves

The aim of conservation management is to maintain a wide variety of appropriate habitats and species and to ensure that the natural habitats of the three counties continue to survive.

Nature reserves are not completely wild, untouched places, but are carefully and sensitively looked after (managed). Over hundreds of years, some wildlife species have adapted to countryside which has been affected by people. For instance, some birds benefit from woods which are regularly coppiced. In these instances, BBONT manages its nature reserves in a traditional manner to recreate these conditions.

Habitats can also change, perhaps by becoming overgrown, sometimes preventing the survival of the species we are trying to protect. For instance, if a valuable grassland site is not cut or grazed, tall vigorous grasses overshadow and smother the smaller, more delicate wild flowers. Seeds from neighbouring woods and hedgerows will be dispersed by wind or animals and some of those landing in the grassland will germinate and grow. As a result, the area will firstly become scrub (a mixture of small trees and shrubs) and eventually woodland. This change from grassland to woodland is an example of the natural process called SUCCESSION. The woodland is the CLIMAX vegetation. The field of grass was probably created many years ago by clearing ancient woodland to provide food for livestock and it represents a SUB-CLIMAX vegetation held in check by grazing.

Unmanaged grassland changes into scrub then into woodland.

How are nature reserves managed?

Nature reserves are managed in a variety of ways:

1. Hay meadows, e.g. Bernwood Meadows (Buckinghamshire)

Unimproved hay meadows support a wide variety of plant and associated insect species. When such meadows are 'improved' by ploughing, draining, fertilizing or reseeding, their interest is lost because the resulting increase in fertility encourages the tougher species to dominate and overshadow the less aggressive wild flowers and grasses.

BBONT manages hay meadows by cutting for hay between July and August. The hay is removed to reduce fertility and to prevent an accumulating blanket of rotting vegetation. Livestock are often put in to graze the subsequent grass growth (known as the 'aftermath'). As selective grazers they help to maintain plant diversity and their footprints provide exposed earth for annual plants to germinate readily.

2. Chalk grassland, e.g. Hartslock (Oxfordshire)

Chalk grasslands occur on thin, dry calcareous soils and often include a great range of wild flowers and insects. Such grasslands have been traditionally managed by the grazing of sheep. BBONT has a flock of sheep that are moved around our various grassland reserves, acting as our living lawn-mowers.

3. Deciduous woodlands, e.g. Moor Copse (Berkshire)

A very great variety of woodland reserves has arisen through various systems of management. The most valuable woods in terms of wildlife are ancient ones that have existed for several centuries and possibly since the last Ice Age. They have trees of different species and ages and tend to have larger numbers of plants and animals associated with them. Most ancient woods were managed as 'coppice with standards' which produced a wide range of sizes of timber suitable for various uses.

For coppicing, trees are chopped down almost to ground level. Their stumps (known as 'coppice stools') regenerate, producing new shoots. Coppiced trees are often multi-stemmed and bushier than normal. Trees left uncut are known as 'standards'.

Areas of 'coppice' benefit wildlife in various ways. When an area of woodland is first coppiced, much more light reaches the woodland floor, encouraging growth of the ground flora, such as bluebells, primroses, violets and yellow archangel, which provides food for caterpillars and other insects. When the coppice has grown tall and dense it will restrict the light reaching the woodland floor. Traditionally a wood would have been divided into compartments with a different section being coppiced each year on a seven to fifteen year cycle, thus ensuring a constant supply of coppice products. An actively coppiced wood is beneficial to wildlife because all stages of the succession from open ground to thicket and old coppice are represented, thus providing habitats for a great variety of plant and animal species.

*Traditional products of
a coppiced woodland.*

Woodland management tasks include:

a. Coppicing.

b. Clearance and maintenance of footpaths.

c. Removal of introduced species, e.g. snowberry, sycamore. Such non-native species are often of low wildlife value and tend to spread rapidly if not controlled. Sycamore is a particularly invasive species in woodlands where it casts very dense shade so that few ground plants are able to grow.

Many native plant species are very valuable to wildlife. Over thousands of years, animals such as insects and other invertebrates have evolved to make use of native plants for food or homes. The invertebrates are then a food source for other wildlife. In comparison, those tree species that have only been here for a few hundred years do not usually have so many invertebrates associated with them.

d. Creation of rides to allow more light to reach the ground. Rides are typically grassy tracks through woodlands. Plants grow and flower here attracting butterflies and other animals. In order to ensure diversity of wild flowers, rides are managed as grasslands, and are mown or grazed.

A woodland ride creates conditions similar to a woodland edge, with grassland, bushes and trees of different ages. This creates a number of habitats which hold a rich variety of wildlife.

e. Maintenance of trees of a variety of ages. This ensures that as older trees die, there are younger trees to replace them.

f. Harvesting coniferous trees which have been planted on some of the sites that are now BBONT reserves. Removing these trees can improve the wildlife on a site, if native deciduous trees grow in their place.

g. Non-intervention. Sometimes a wood is allowed to develop naturally to become a future 'wildwood'.

4. Ponds, e.g. Henry Stephen/C.S. Lewis Nature Reserve (Oxfordshire)

Most ponds have been created to provide water for livestock or through extraction of stone, gravel or clay. A pond is a temporary landscape feature and naturally becomes filled with dead plant matter and silt. Left for long enough it will become a marsh and eventually dry out completely. Ponds provide valuable habitat for amphibians and many invertebrates and birds. Managing ponds entails occasional dredging, limiting excessive plant growth and cutting back of overhanging trees.

5. Heathland, e.g. Inkpen Common (Berkshire)

Heathland is the type of vegetation usually found on poor, acidic soils. It is dominated by heathers, with a variety of fine grasses and wild flowers. Natural succession leads to invasion by birch followed by other tree species.

Traditionally many heathland areas were managed as common land and local people had common rights to graze livestock, cut wood and peat for fuel and gather bracken and heather for bedding. Livestock maintained the heathland because the grazing animals kept shrubs and trees from invading. Another traditional method of management was burning. The heather regenerated, providing new shoots for livestock to graze. Management of these areas today entails controlling birch and also removing bracken which tends to spread and dominate heathland. Some areas of scrub are left to provide cover for birds.

6. Bogs, e.g. Owlsmoor Bog and Heath (Berkshire)

Bogs are wet areas that develop on poorly drained soils and are dominated by sphagnum mosses. Some interesting insectivorous plants may grow among them. There are now very few bogs in our three counties. Management entails removal of invading scrub (often birch) and maintaining high water levels to prevent bogs from drying out.

7. Hedgerows, e.g. Tuckmill Meadow (Oxfordshire)

As more areas of woodland have disappeared from the countryside, hedgerows have become increasingly important, providing valuable habitats for nesting birds, small mammals and insects. Hedgerows are linear 'woodland edge' habitats, acting as corridors between patches of woodland and as refuges for some species that forage in open fields, such as predatory insects that eat aphids. Hedgerows can be hundreds of years old. A method of determining the age of a hedge is to count the number of species in 30 yards, not including climbers such as honeysuckle. The number of species = the age of the hedge in centuries.

Traditional management involved laying hedges about every fifteen years. This activity promotes new growth and in the long term provides a thick, stockproof hedge that is also very valuable to wildlife. Coppicing is another form of traditional hedge management.

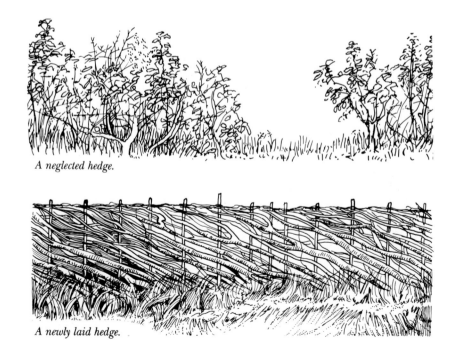

A neglected hedge.

A newly laid hedge.

8. Man-made wildlife sites, e.g. College Lake Wildlife Centre (Buckinghamshire)
Not all our nature reserves have arisen through traditional management over many years. Some have been created through much more recent and seemingly destructive human activities. Our list of nature reserves includes ponds created through clay extraction for brick-making, old railway lines, an old sand and gravel quarry and disused gravel pits. When such sites are left undisturbed for a number of years they can develop into valuable habitats of great wildlife interest. It is possible to create particular types of habitat by careful land management, planting appropriate plants or creating ideal conditions for the seeds to germinate. One BBONT site, Wells Farm in Oxfordshire, is run as a working farm, but also has field margins, hedgerows and ponds for wildlife. In future, created habitats could provide new sites for wildlife throughout the country.

Who manages the BBONT nature reserves?

Managing nature reserves is a considerable responsibility and involves a great deal of time, expertise and money. Staff reserve officers are responsible for ensuring the smooth running of the nature reserves. Each reserve has a volunteer reserve manager and a team of wardens who keep an eye on the site and carry out any necessary management work. Management plans and schedules of work are produced in order to ensure each site will be managed appropriately both now and in the future.

Visiting nature reserves

We welcome visitors to the nature reserves described in this book. You may visit most of the reserves at any time but it is necessary to obtain a permit to visit those described in the 'restricted access' section. We hope that you will enjoy our reserves and that you will return to visit them at different times of the year.

Nature reserves are carefully and sensitively managed wildlife sites. In order to have a safe and enjoyable visit, please remember the following:

1. Go properly equipped. Take stout footwear, waterproofs and sensible clothing.
2. Remember to take maps and instructions on how to get to the nature reserve. Many nature reserves have wildlife walk leaflets which guide the visitor around the site. These are available from BBONT Headquarters or The Wildlife Shop.
3. Always take notice of any signs warning of danger.
4. BBONT nature reserves are not as accessible as country parks. If you have mobility difficulties or need to know details of disabled access, please contact BBONT Headquarters.
5. ALWAYS tell someone where you are going and what time you can be expected back.

In order to safeguard the wildlife of BBONT's nature reserves:

1. Please do not remove any plants or animals from reserves.
2. Please keep to the paths wherever possible.
3. Close all gates and avoid trespass or disturbance to adjacent property.
4. Take care to avoid disturbing birds or other animals especially during the spring and early summer when they are breeding.
5. Guard against fire risk. Plantations, woodlands and heathlands are highly inflammable.
6. Please take litter away with you.
7. Sheep and cattle are often used to graze reserves for the benefit of the grassland plants. Please avoid disturbing these animals.
8. Dogs disturb wildlife. They are prohibited on some reserves and are only allowed into others on a lead. Please take notice of all instructions.

BBONT accepts no responsibility for any loss, injury or damage, howsoever caused, which may be sustained while visiting the reserves described in this book.

When to visit nature reserves

Some nature reserves are at their best at particular times of year. Below is a general guide.
Woodlands – all year round (particularly spring).
Lakes – all year round.
Heathland – spring to autumn.
Meadows – late spring/early summer.

Educational activities on nature reserves

In 1994 BBONT opened the doors to its first **Environmental Education Centre**. Fully funded by Shanks & McEwan, the centre is adjacent to a small nature reserve and surrounded by a wildlife garden on their landfill site at Calvert, Buckinghamshire. It has a fully equipped classroom and a qualified Education Officer is on hand to assist teachers with a wide range of environmental activities for all ages and abilities. Other less formal groups such as guides, cubs, Watch groups etc. are also welcome to use the centre.

To book a visit write to The Education Officer, Calvert Environmental Education Centre, Shanks & McEwan, Brackley Lane, Calvert, Buckinghamshire, MK18 2EW, or telephone 01296 730814.

Taking groups of children to nature reserves

BBONT also has two nature reserves where a paid warden is available to help and guide schools around the reserve:

Warburg Reserve near Henley. To book a visit phone 01491 641727.
College Lake Wildlife Centre near Tring. Phone 01296 668805.

The **Henry Stephen/C.S. Lewis Nature Reserve** in Oxford, although it has no warden on site, is used extensively by local schools. It has an education hut and pond-dipping equipment which can be booked by phoning BBONT HQ on 01865 775476.

Many of BBONT's other nature reserves are suitable for schools and other groups to use, but it is important to follow these guidelines:

1. Teachers and group leaders are strongly advised to make a prior visit to the nature reserve before attending with their group.
2. There should **always** be at least one adult to every 10 children. There must be a minimum of two adults with any group.
3. To avoid more than one group arriving at a reserve on a particular day, please give at least one week's notice before visiting.
4. All groups and leaders should comply with the 1992 Children's Act.
5. Educational visits to nature reserves should be enjoyable so that children leave the reserves with an increased understanding of the environment and the need to conserve it. In addition, please encourage children to treat the nature reserve with care and respect for its wildlife at all times.

Using this book

This book has been carefully planned for easy use. There are three sections:

Visitor nature reserves
Open access nature reserves
Restricted access nature reserves

The nature reserves are listed alphabetically in each section. Each reserve account gives details of the reserve's size, nearest towns, location and access, followed by a description and brief information about the management of the reserve. Months when wild flowers can be expected to be in bloom are indicated by the month numbers in brackets, e.g. ragged-Robin (5–7) flowers from May to July. Reserve maps show boundaries, where to park, where to enter the reserves and the main footpaths and habitats.

A diagram of Berkshire, Buckinghamshire and Oxfordshire is shown next to the heading for each nature reserve, with an arrow. The tip of this arrow indicates the approximate location of the reserve within the three counties. A more detailed colour map is included as an insert with this book, and shows all the BBONT nature reserves, along with main roads and towns.

The following symbols are used to indicate special features and the main wildlife interest for each reserve:

SS SI	Site of Special Scientific Interest	🦋	Insects
📖	Leaflet available	🐦	Birds
⌂	Visitors centre	🐾	Mammals, amphibians, reptiles
WC	Toilets	🍄	Fungi
♿	Disabled access	🌼	Plants

Visitor nature reserves

These are reserves which have interesting wildlife or views for much of the year, walks for visitors, some parking and reasonable access to the site. Each of these reserves is worth travelling away from your local area to visit. The sites vary from woodlands and heathlands to lakes and bogs. In addition a meadow, best in late spring/early summer, has been included as an example of a flower-rich grassland.

Open access nature reserves

These sites are also suitable for visitors, but may be spectacular for a only a small proportion of the year, have limited parking or may be less accessible. However, they are still worth visiting, especially if local to you.

Restricted access nature reserves

These sites are restricted for a variety of reasons. Some sites are extremely susceptible to trampling or disturbance, and in other cases the owner may wish to restrict the number of visitors to his or her land.

To obtain details of these sites and permits to visit, please send a stamped, addressed envelope to the nearest BBONT county office at least four weeks before your visit requesting details and a permit. Please include the date you intend to visit the reserve.

Grid references

The locations of the reserves are given as grid references on the relevant Ordnance Survey 1:50,000 scale Landranger series maps. The Trust has reserves located on the following maps: No. 151 (Stratford-upon-Avon), No. 152 (Northampton and Milton Keynes), No. 163 (Cheltenham and Cirencester), No. 164 (Oxford), No. 165 (Aylesbury and Leighton Buzzard), No. 174 (Newbury and Wantage), No. 175 (Reading and Windsor) and No. 176 (West London).

The reserves can be located by using the six figure grid reference number given for each site. In case you are unfamiliar with this reference system it is explained below:

e.g. SU 725884

SU – Britain has been divided up into a grid system of 100 km by 100 km squares. Each square is given two letters, e.g. SP, SU. These tell you which square you are in. They are usually written in the corner of the map, but sometimes, if an Ordnance Survey map covers two of these grid squares, these letters will appear in other places around the map's perimeter.

725884 – Divide this number into two groups of three digits, i.e. 725 and 884. The first set of three, 725, refers to the numbers going across the bottom of the map. 725 really means 72 and five tenths. Follow the numbers across the

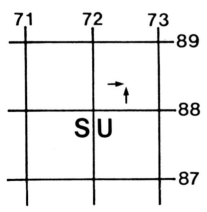

bottom (or top) of the map until you find number 72. Go five tenths of a square further on and stop. Put your finger on this point.

The second set of three numbers, 884, refers to the numbers running up the sides of the map. 884 means 88 and four tenths. Follow the numbers up the sides until you find number 88. Go four tenths of a square further up and stop. Put your finger on this point.

Move your fingers vertically upwards (or downwards) and horizontally across until they meet. This is the location of the reserve.

List of abbreviations used in this handbook

BTCV   British Trust for Conservation Volunteers
EN   English Nature
SSSI   Site of Special Scientific Interest (i.e. a site of national importance in terms of its wildlife or geology).

BBONT addresses and telephone numbers

BBONT Headquarters

3 Church Cowley Road
Oxford
OX4 3JR
Tel: 01865 775476 – Fax: 01865 711301

BBONT Berkshire Office

Dinton Pastures Country Park
Davis Street
Hurst
Reading
RG10 0TH
Tel: 01734 341721 – Fax: 01734 344721

The Wildlife Shop and Wildlife Information Service

53 St Mary's Street
Wallingford
OX10 0ER
Tel. and Fax: 01491 824944

Calvert Environmental Education Centre

Shanks & McEwan
Brackley Lane
Calvert
Buckinghamshire
MK18 2EW
Tel: 01296 730814

Visitor nature reserves

Baynes Reserve
Bernwood Meadows
Bowdown Woods
Broadmoor Bottom
Chinnor Hill
College Lake Wildlife Centre
The Cothill Reserves:
Dry Sandford Pit, Hitchcopse Pit,
Lashford Lane Fen & Parsonage Moor
Dancersend & The Crong Meadow
Decoy Heath
Finemere Wood
Foxholes
Grangelands
Henry Stephen/C.S. Lewis Reserve
Inkpen Common
Little Linford Wood
Loddon Reserve
Moor Copse
Owlsmoor Bog & Heath
Rushbeds Wood & Lapland Farm
Stony Stratford
Sydlings Copse & College Pond
Tuckmill Meadow
The Warburg Reserve
Wells Farm

Baynes Reserve

OS sheet 174; SU 511651

Nearest town Newbury

An ancient woodland, 16 hectares (40 acres) in extent, part of the Bowdown Woods and Chamberhouse Woods SSSI. BBONT has owned the freehold since 1983. The reserve is situated a short distance from Bowdown Woods reserve (see page 28)

Location

From Thatcham, just to the east of Newbury take the (unclassified) road south past Thatcham Station, over the River Kennet, and as the road rises to Crookham Common take Bury's Bank Road (a narrow right fork) which soon meets Greenham Common Airfield. After ½ mile, turn right down a gravel track (SU 511649) which leads past Thatched Lodge to a small car park. The reserve is in front of you.

Access

Open to the public along the paths. Dogs must be kept on a lead.

Description

This is ancient woodland, which has existed for many centuries, perhaps since the return of trees at the end of the last Ice Age. However, this does not mean that it is wildwood untouched or unmanaged by man. No British woodland is!

The reserve has two stream valleys converging to the north-east. Cutting down through layers of gravels and clays, these valleys provide several distinct habitats. The higher, well-drained slopes have rather acidic soil, supporting birch and rowan with patches of oak and hazel. Honeysuckle (flowering 6–9, with berries 8–9), foxglove (6–8), bramble (5–9), bluebells (4–6), bracken and several species of fern can also be found. Further down the slopes, the wetter and richer soils are marked by alder and hazel. Look here for the unusual five-ways-facing flowers of town-hall-clock or moschatel (4–5), cuckoo pint or lords-and-ladies (flowering 4–5, with red berries 7–8) which is perhaps more familiar in hedgerows, and wood-sorrel (4–5), folding its leaves down in rain. Springs emerge on the slopes creating 'wet flushes', marked in April and May by splashes of flowering opposite-leaved golden-saxifrage (4–7).

These woodlands are alive with birdsong. The nightingale sings here from late April to late June (it likes dense low cover such as coppice or scrub to nest in and will desert woods which grow too 'leggy').

Roe and muntjac deer are present, and dormice sometimes leave evidence of their activities: look out for honeysuckle neatly stripped of bark 1–2½ metres from the ground – dormice use the bark as nesting material. The handsome white admiral and the majestic purple emperor butterflies are on the wing here in July and August. The visitor will see many species of dragonfly – 15 in all have been recorded. Some breed in the streams but most fly in from nearby ponds.

Management

The old coppicing regime which regularly opens up a wood and creates diversity has been continued on a modest scale.

24

Baynes Reserve

OS sheet 174; SU 511651

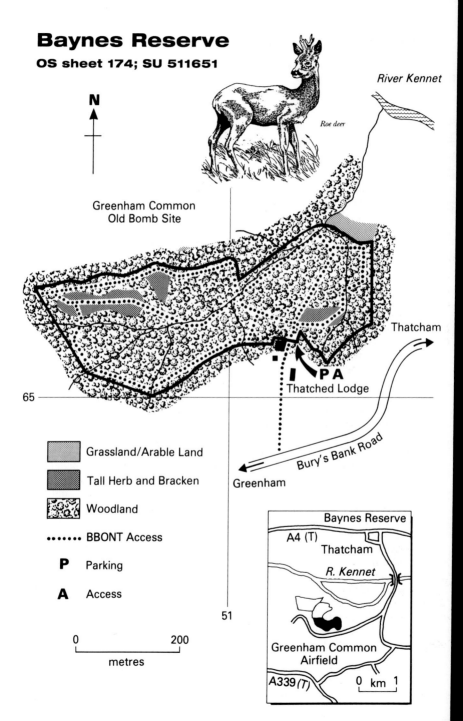

N

River Kennet

Roe deer

Greenham Common
Old Bomb Site

Thatcham

PA
Thatched Lodge

65

Bury's Bank Road

Greenham

▦ Grassland/Arable Land

▦ Tall Herb and Bracken

▦ Woodland

••••••• BBONT Access

P Parking

A Access

51

0 ⸺⸺⸺ 200

metres

Baynes Reserve

A4 (T)
Thatcham

R. Kennet

Greenham Common
Airfield

A339 (T)   0 km 1

Bernwood Meadows
OS sheets 164 & 165; SP 606111

Nearest towns Oxford and Thame

Two wild flower meadows bordered by hedges, some of which are ancient. There are also two small ponds. The reserve totals 7.3 hectares (18.3 acres). An SSSI, it was bought by BBONT in 1981.

Location

From Headington roundabout on Oxford's eastern ring road, take the road north past the crematorium. Turn right, cross the B4027 and proceed to Stanton St John. Take the first left in the village. Fork left at the road junction at Menmarsh, and after ¾ mile there is a small car park on the right.

Access
Open to the public but please keep to the two footpaths from mid-April until the hay has been cut, to avoid damaging the flowers and disturbing the butterflies. Dogs are not allowed when stock are grazing, and must be kept on leads at all times.

Description
Although medieval 'ridge and furrow' is to be seen, especially in the western meadow, the fields have seemingly escaped the plough in more recent times. Equally, there seems to have been little use of artificial fertilizers which encourage coarser grasses at the expense of other plants. (Certainly for the past 25 years at least the only manuring has been from grazing livestock.) As a result of this and the hay and grazing regime, wild flowers have prospered. Over 100 plant species have been recorded here, including 23 different wild grasses. There is a good display of green-winged orchids (flowering 5–6). Adder's-tongue, a plant typical of ancient meadows, can also be seen.

The communities of plants reflect differences in the soil below. The wide stripes of the medieval ridge and furrow were created by the ox teams ploughing down one side, turning at the 'headland' and ploughing back up the other, throwing the soil inwards on both passes to create the ridge. In early summer buttercups colour the drier ridges but are absent from the furrows. By contrast, the furrows with their damper soil promote scattered growths of rushes and other damp-loving plants which are absent from the ridges.

The patch of lush green grass with few flowers, almost due south of the car park, contrasts with the rest of the meadow. The ground has clearly been disturbed and fertilized here.

Butterflies and other insects add further interest to these attractive meadows.

Management
The hay is mown in July, followed by grazing of the regrowth. Some blackthorn hedges are managed by being cut in rotation at intervals of many years in order to produce a range of ages of blackthorn. The hedge along the road has been laid in the traditional manner. The willows around the larger pond are pollarded.

Bernwood Meadows

OS sheets 164 & 165; SP 606111

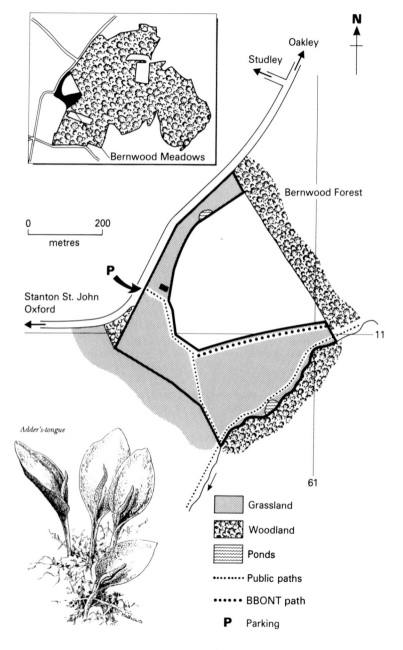

Bernwood Meadows

N

Oakley

Studley

Bernwood Forest

0   200
metres

P

Stanton St. John
Oxford

11

61

Adder's-tongue

Grassland

Woodland

Ponds

•••••••• Public paths

•••••• BBONT path

P   Parking

Bowdown Woods

OS sheet 174; SU 501655

Nearest town Newbury

A varied nature reserve of 22 hectares (55 acres), of which 20 hectares (50 acres) lie within the Bowdown and Chamberhouse Woods SSSI. The reserve was bought by BBONT in 1984.

Location
Leave Newbury southwards on the A34. At the roundabout at the top of the hill turn left to the village of Greenham, and drive for about 1½ miles along Bury's Bank Road until you reach a small track on the left, with a sign saying 'strictly no admittance'. This refers to the gravel workings further down the track. Take this track to a small car park on the right.

Access
Open to the public along the paths. Dogs are not allowed.

Description
The reserve stretches for half a mile along a wooded slope which runs between a gravelly plateau and the River Kennet. London clay lies below the gravel and has outcrops along the lower slopes. Spring-fed streams have cut numerous sharp valleys in the slope and there are also areas of seepage.

On this varied geological stage, vegetation creates its own scenery. There is dry heathland on the plateau and some patches of oak woodland with wild cherry and mountain ash (rowan) to be seen. The brilliant red berries of the latter are eagerly taken by birds in autumn. There is hazel and scattered birch and, on wetter ground, stands of coppiced willow and alder. More coppiced woodland, this time of ash and field maple, occupies the lower, clay areas. There are also areas of grassland and two ponds. Solomon's-seal (flowering 5–6) is one of the many spring flowers to interest the visitor.

The wet ground makes tracking relatively easy. The droppings of fox, roe deer and muntjac deer can be expected. Roe deer are rather secretive, but clues of their presence can be seen around the rutting season (June – August). Look for trees with frayed bark which have been anointed with scent as territory markers and used for scraping antlers free of velvet. During rutting, the roe buck gives out throaty grunts. The muntjac often gives a loud, unexpected doglike bark from cover, surprising visitors.

Dormice and slow-worms also live on the reserve, and white admiral and silver-washed fritillary butterflies are present. The purple hairstreak is also to be seen, though perhaps less frequently as it tends to keep to the upper branches of the oak trees. There are many moth species and a rare slug for the specialist.

Management
Rides and paths have been opened up, some areas have been coppiced, invading sycamore has been controlled and the area of heather on the brow of the reserve has been extended.

28

Bowdown Woods

OS sheet 174; SU 501655

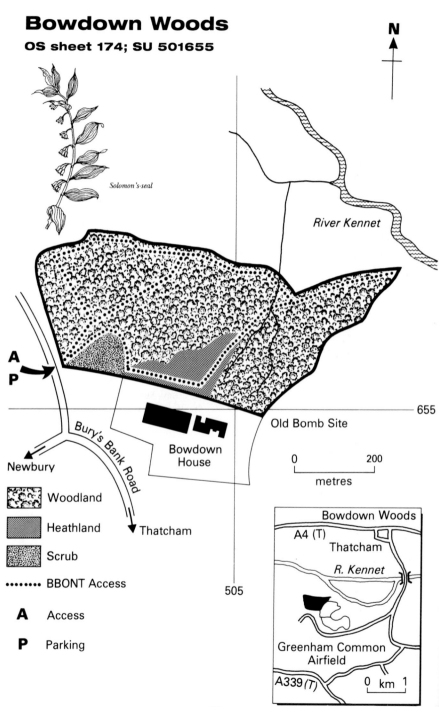

Solomon's-seal

N

River Kennet

655

Old Bomb Site

Newbury

Bury's Bank Road

Bowdown House

0   200
metres

Thatcham

505

Woodland

Heathland

Scrub

BBONT Access

A   Access

P   Parking

Bowdown Woods

A4 (T)

Thatcham

R. Kennet

Greenham Common Airfield

A339 (T)   0   km   1

Broadmoor Bottom

OS sheet 175; SU 853628

Nearest towns Sandhurst, Bracknell and Camberley

A mosaic of broadleaved and pine woodland, scrub, dry and wet heathland and ponds. The reserve is in three blocks. One block is south of Rackstraw Lane and 2.75 hectares (6.6 acres) in area. The other two are north of Rackstraw Lane, divided by a by-pass, and together are 8.03 hectares (19.3 acres) in area. Most of the reserve lies within the Broadmoor to Bagshot Woods and Heaths SSSI, and it is managed by BBONT in agreement with Broadmoor Hospital.

Location

From the centre of Sandhurst take the A321 east and turn left at a roundabout on to the A3095. Cross two roundabouts until open land appears to the left. Drive for just over ¼ mile and take the left turning before the next roundabout. Park next to the electricity sub-station at SU 850629 (OWLSMOOR BOG AND HEATH reserve can also be visited from here; see page 68). The map shows the access points.

Access

The reserve is open to the public, except for the area of woodland north of Rackstraw Lane.

Description

Heathland needs to be treasured today. Over 80% of it has been lost over the country as a whole. This fragment, crossed as it is by pylons and edged by housing sprawl, is a last refuge in the neighbourhood for lizards, heathers and woodlark.

Heathland came into existence when woodland was cleared long ago in late Stone Age and Bronze Age times. The heathland here became part of the Royal Windsor Forest, a hunting domain. Grazing and cutting of heather and gorse, by those with local common rights, kept it open for the chase. However early in the last century, field enclosures ate into the open heath and there was much planting of Scots pine. Grazing and cutting declined, allowing trees to invade (the wooded areas were open before 1871). Housing sprawl then began to take hold. By 1931, Broadmoor Bottom was one of the last fragments of the once extensive Bagshot Heath and in 1971 new housing to the south eroded it further.

Thus, of the range of closely interlinked habitats to be seen on the reserve, the open heathland and valley bog areas are of particular interest as relics of former times. In the valley bog grow bog asphodel (flowering 7–8) and bog myrtle (catkins 4–5), together with the 'insect-eating' round-leaved sundew (6–8). Heather occupies drier soil.

There are many dragonflies, and one notable butterfly is the silver-studded blue. The handsome day-flying emperor moth might also be seen in May. Woodlark and stonechat are amongst the birds recorded as nesting here.

Management

The open heath must be kept clear of scrub and trees which will invade if given the opportunity.

Broadmoor Bottom

OS sheet 175; SU 853628

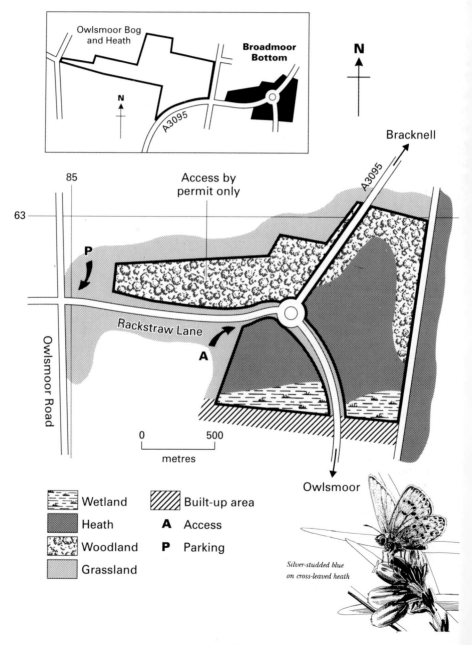

Silver-studded blue
on cross-leaved heath

Legend:
- Wetland
- Heath
- Woodland
- Grassland
- Built-up area
- **A** Access
- **P** Parking

Chinnor Hill

OS sheet 165; SP 766002

Nearest towns Chinnor, Princes Risborough and Thame

A reserve of 28 hectares (70 acres) of chalk slope, with woodland, scrub and grassland. It is an SSSI, owned by BBONT since 1965. In addition to its wildlife interest there are two Bronze Age burial mounds and three ancient sunken tracks down the slopes.

Location

From Chinnor take the unclassified road up the scarp and take the first left turn back towards Bledlow Ridge. As the road goes round to the right, turn left again into Hill Top Lane and drive to the car park at the end. The reserve is in front of you.

Access

Open to the public. There is a network of public footpaths and bridleways, including a length of the Upper Icknield Way.

Description

The reserve is situated on the Chiltern escarpment and carries soils of two kinds, clay-with-flints at the top and shallow, quickly draining chalky soil on the slopes. There is an area of woodland with oak and ash, and small areas of mature open-floored beech woodland at the top of the hill. These apart, the whole area was once open grazing land, with juniper growing on the steep slopes.

Earlier this century, livestock were removed and only rabbits grazed the site. In the 1950s, the rabbit population was severely reduced by myxomatosis. With grazing pressure removed, a dense mixed scrub of hawthorn, wild privet, traveller's-joy, spindle, buckthorn and other woody species gradually grew up, invading large areas and killing some, but not all, of the juniper.

There are wild roses in the grassland, dog rose (flowering 6–7) and sweet briar (6–7) with apple-scented leaves, to the south of Icknield Way.

The open chalk grassland carries typical wild flowers, such as common rock-rose (flowering 5–9), wild thyme (5–8) and Chiltern gentian (8–9). Look also for the pyramidal straw-coloured flower of the very prickly carline thistle (7–10).

As is to be expected from such a large area of scrub, the reserve has large populations of nesting birds, including four different species of warblers. In autumn and winter the areas of scrub provide a rich larder of berries for birds of the thrush family, such as redwings and fieldfares.

With its fine views over the southern end of the Vale of Aylesbury this reserve is worth a visit at any time of year.

Management

Some scrub has been cleared and it is hoped to clear more in the future. A proportion of the hazel has been coppiced. The grassland area at the summit is grazed each year by BBONT's sheep.

Chinnor Hill

OS sheet 165; SP 766002

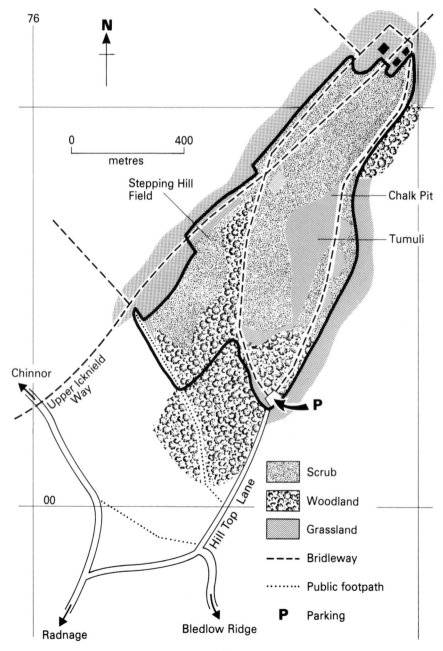

76

N

0   400
metres

Stepping Hill
Field

Chalk Pit

Tumuli

Chinnor

Upper Icknield Way

Hill Top Lane

00

Scrub

Woodland

Grassland

– – – Bridleway

.... Public footpath

P Parking

Radnage

Bledlow Ridge

College Lake Wildlife Centre

OS sheet 165; SP 933139

Nearest town Tring

A worked-out chalk quarry which has been restored as a wildlife centre, College Lake is a joint project between BBONT and Castle Cement (Pitstone) Ltd. It is 40 hectares (100 acres) in area including a 10 hectare lake. Part of the quarry has been designated an SSSI for its geological importance.

Location

From the roundabout on the A41 just to the west of Tring, take the B488 for 2½ miles. At Bulbourne, cross the canal bridge. The reserve entrance is a further 275 metres on the left-hand side.

Access

All visitors must have a permit. The site is open to the general public daily, 10 am to 5 pm, with permits from the Warden's Office on the reserve. BBONT members can visit at any time with an annual permit from the same office or from the Conservation Officer, Castle Cement (Pitstone) Ltd, Pitstone, Leighton Buzzard, Beds LU7 9AR. (Please include a stamped addressed envelope.) The majority of the bird hides are accessible to people in wheelchairs. Concrete paths lead to the hides from the car park. There is a wildlife walks leaflet to guide the visitor around the reserve. This is available at the site itself or from BBONT headquarters.

Description

This is an excellent example of creative conservation in action. The rehabilitation plans have been devised jointly by BBONT, supplying expertise, voluntary labour and wardens, and Castle Cement, providing funding and machinery.

The project began in 1985 with the creation of a mixture of contrasting habitats. The reserve now incorporates a lake, several large islands, shingle beaches, floating nesting rafts, bird observation hides and a visitor/information centre.

The largest single feature of the reserve is the lake. This was created through a 'shape-as-you-go' plan while quarrying was still taking place. The lake's features were marked out and shaped by bulldozers with minimal disruption to the quarrying process. In 1991, the pumps which kept the workings dry were switched off and the lake allowed to fill up naturally. Parts of the lake are now over 7 metres deep.

Safe breeding sites have been provided by anchored rafts on the lake and the islands at its centre. The islands were created using hundreds of tonnes of shingle. A shallow beach has been created to allow easy access for wildfowl. A feeding area has been provided by a shingle bank, rising barely above the water level when full. This is close to the Beach Island, but separated from it by a shallow, narrow channel.

The whole local area is particularly important for its birdlife, and the lake is an addition to the Tring complex of open waters which are famous among bird watchers.

A variety of waders, terns and other species are regularly seen on passage. Breeding birds include lapwing, redshank and little ringed plover. The latter was seldom seen in Britain before World War II, but in 1938 a pair nested at one of the Tring reservoirs and since then the species has become established. Hundreds now nest at gravel pits throughout central and eastern England. Its eggs are laid in a simple scrape in the gravel, and the chicks are well camouflaged. Nevertheless, predation by crows and other plunderers is heavy.

The birdlife of the lake can be enjoyed from a number of hides placed around its edge. These provide contrasting views of Beach Island, the open water and the shallows where waders can be observed.

Two smaller areas of water exist in the reserve. The first is a dyke and pool system that runs around the southern woodland area. This was used as a drainage point when quarrying was taking place. The water level of this system can be controlled by the reserve's conservation officer. The system is flooded in winter creating a marshy area for wintering wildfowl such as wigeon, teal and gadwall. The marsh has been planted with willows, rushes, reeds and aquatic plants. It is particularly important because marsh habitats are in decline in many parts of the country. In spring and summer, water levels are lowered. This allows plants at the margins to flower. These include marsh-marigold (flowering 3–8), cuckooflower (4–6), and ragged-Robin (5–8). The dropping water level also reveals muddy margins which provide a source of invertebrates for waders. Willow warblers, snipe and kingfishers are frequently seen near the marshy area, while in summer dragonflies and damselflies dart between bulrushes (6–7), bur-reeds (6–8) and mare's-tail (6–7). Mare's-tail is a favourite food of water voles which can occasionally be seen scurrying along the banks.

The second stretch of water is Molly's Pond, a specially created hollow which catches 'run-off' water from the higher ground to the north-east of the lake. To avoid problems with large amounts of run-off, an overflow pipe feeds from the pond down to the reedbed in the marshy shallows of the lake.

Thousands of native species trees and shrubs have been planted. There are two areas of woodland, one in the southern part of the reserve, surrounded by dykes and the lake, and the other bordering on the lake's northern and eastern sides. The former, College Wood, has 4 hectares of mixed native trees and shrubs, including beech, ash, oak, cherry, hawthorn and bramble. Wide grassy rides divide this into compartments, designed to attract wild flowers and butterflies.

Planting began in 1989 and was completed in two seasons. Although well-established, the woodland is still young and requires many years to develop fully. As this happens, the diversity of wildlife found here will increase.

A large area of the reserve is open grassland, both grazed and ungrazed, with chalk banks edging the reserve on three sides. These banks are grazed where possible

Teal

to help stabilise erosion. Rare-breed sheep at the reserve are tough enough to survive on the scarce vegetation on the slopes. Their grazing and climbing disturbs the surface allowing more vegetation to take hold. On the flatter grassland, their grazing controls the coarse grasses which would shade out the more delicate wild flowers.

Directly below the Arable Weed Centre, the steep banks are constantly eroding. Surprisingly, colt's-foot (2–4) and kidney vetch (4–9) thrive here, the latter attracting butterflies such as the small blue.

Warden's Bank, near the entrance, has an unusual history. The ancient flower-rich turf was originally from Pitstone Hill. However, in 1988 quarrying threatened its existence, so it was cut into blocks and transported by volunteers to a west-facing bank on the reserve. It is now thriving, retaining its host of wild flowers – cowslips (4–5), thyme (6–7), milkwort (5–9) and numerous orchids. Even its anthills were retained. The bank is particularly attractive to butterflies and grasshoppers.

The reserve's hay meadows are cut in summer after the wild flowers have bloomed and the young birds have flown away. The regrowth or 'aftermath' is then grazed to check invasive weeds and recycle nutrients. Hares can be seen boxing here in March, and skylarks and meadow pipits can be heard in summer.

Before quarrying began in the late 1960s, Castle Cement removed much of the topsoil of the site and stockpiled it. The soil contained a huge number of seeds, some of which had been dormant for many years. In order to investigate this, in 1987, the Arable Weed Project began. The Project started growing traditional wheat and other cereals under traditional conditions, together with once common cornfield flowers.

Crop rotation of 'old-fashioned' cereals is practised. The plots are left fallow the year after cereals are cropped. The rare-breed sheep graze the fallow ground. One of the aims of the Project is to grow wild flowers in a traditional cornfield setting. With the extensive use of chemicals in modern farming, cornfields now lack the blaze of colour provided by the wild flowers seen as weeds by farmers. Many of these wild flowers have become rare and are in need of conservation.

At the centre of the reserve is the Susan Cowdy Centre. This contains some, but not all, of the reserve's fossil collection. Bones of mammoths, lions and bears have been found at the reserve. The landscape was probably similar to the African Savannah, but with a similar climate to today. The entire length of the quarry bank is a designated geological SSSI. Circular patterns created by temperature extremes in the tundra permafrost at the end of the last Ice Age can be seen in cross-section. A number of the site's fossils can also be seen at the County Museum in Aylesbury.

Management

The quarry banks are grazed by BBONT's sponsored flock of sheep and other rare breeds owned by the warden. A sheep breeding programme has been established to promote interest in and further the work of the Rare Breeds Survival Trust. The hay meadows are cut in late summer and the Slade is grazed late in the year to control vegetation. New projects are being carried out at the reserve all the time. If you are interested in helping, please contact the warden.

College Lake Wildlife Centre
OS sheet 165; SP 933139

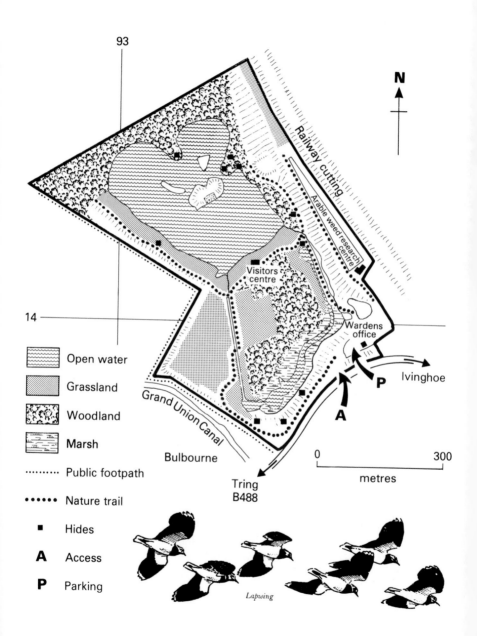

Open water

Grassland

Woodland

Marsh

.... Public footpath

•••••• Nature trail

■ Hides

A Access

P Parking

Railway cutting

Arable weed research centre

Visitors centre

Wardens office

Ivinghoe

Grand Union Canal

Bulbourne

Tring B488

0   300

metres

Lapwing

The Cothill Reserves Dry Sandford Pit

OS sheet 164; SU 467997

Nearest towns Oxford and Abingdon

An old stone and sand quarry, the eastern part of which is an SSSI as a result of both its ecological and its geological importance. Eight hectares (20 acres) in area. BBONT bought the freehold in 1979.

Location
The reserve lies in Cothill village, 2 miles north-west of Abingdon. It is best approached by turning off Wootton Road (B4017) almost directly opposite the garage which marks its junction with the Boars Hill/Foxcombe Hill road. Very soon after entering Cothill, turn left beyond the Dry Sandford turning into a lay-by which leads up a slope to a small car park. The reserve is in front of you over a stile.

Access
Open to the public, but the fen area is a fragile habitat and should be avoided. Please do not attempt to collect fossils from the cliff face. Keep dogs under control and on a lead especially when BBONT's sheep are grazing. There is a wildlife walk booklet available from BBONT HQ to guide visitors around the site.

WARNING: keep clear of the cliff overhangs which may suddenly give way!

Description
Largely an old sand and stone quarry which has been partly filled in. Low cliffs remain on the northeast side. These exposed areas are one of Britain's best sites for burrowing bees and wasps.

Springs feed part of the old quarry floor and there is shallow open water surrounded by fen. The stream flowing from these springs forms a long pond and then joins Sandford Brook which runs along the western boundary of the reserve. The area next to the brook is mainly woodland. Apart from two small ponds, the rest is grassland with scrub and tree cover in places.

The fen area and surrounding area have been partly colonised by various species of willow, birch and alder. Orchids include early marsh-orchids (flowering 5–7), common spotted-orchids (5–7) and a large colony of marsh helleborines (7–8). These wet areas provide a habitat for a wide range of wildlife, including frogs, toads, newts, and grass snakes, while birds include moorhen, kingfisher and green woodpecker. Dragonflies and damselflies are common.

The turf areas have many wild flowers. On the bare rocks and sandy soil below the cliff a 'heath' of lichens can be seen. In autumn many fungi are present.

Glow-worms are seen on summer nights, and the penetrating song of the great green bush-cricket is something to listen for, from July to October. The reserve is also home to a large colony of marbled white butterflies. These are on the wing in July.

Management
Scrub growth around the pond and fen areas is checked while the BBONT sheep graze the grassy areas and limit the spread of coarse herbage.

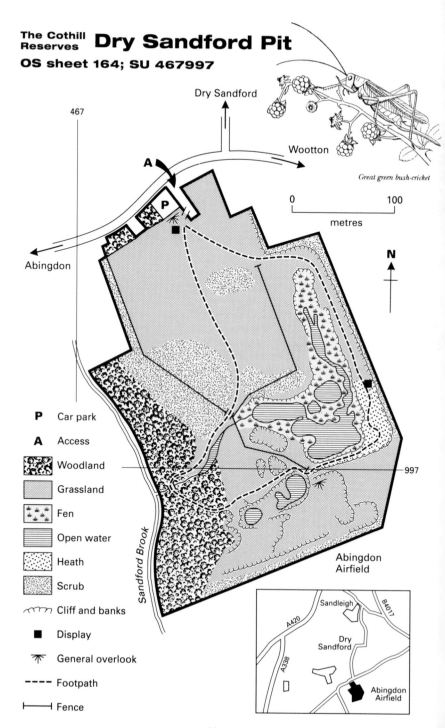

The Cothill Reserves **Dry Sandford Pit**

OS sheet 164; SU 467997

Dry Sandford

Wootton

Great green bush-cricket

467

A

P

Abingdon

0   100

metres

N

997

P   Car park

A   Access

Woodland

Grassland

Fen

Open water

Heath

Scrub

Cliff and banks

■   Display

General overlook

- - - - Footpath

⊢——⊣ Fence

Sandford Brook

Abingdon Airfield

Sandleigh

Dry Sandford

Abingdon Airfield

A420

B4017

A338

39

Hitchcopse Pit

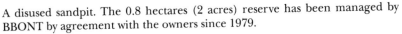

OS sheet 164; SU 452996

Nearest towns Abingdon and Oxford

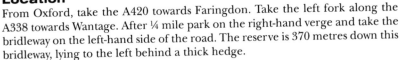

A disused sandpit. The 0.8 hectares (2 acres) reserve has been managed by BBONT by agreement with the owners since 1979.

Location
From Oxford, take the A420 towards Faringdon. Take the left fork along the A338 towards Wantage. After ¼ mile park on the right-hand verge and take the bridleway on the left-hand side of the road. The reserve is 370 metres down this bridleway, lying to the left behind a thick hedge.

Access
Open to the public. Dogs must be kept on a lead. Beware of the danger of rock falls around the lips of the pit.

Description
This long-disused sandpit is full of wildlife interest. It is close to Frilford Heath, a famous entomological site with exceptional numbers of ant, bee and wasp species. It complements DRY SANDFORD PIT reserve (page 38), as it satisfies the requirements of species which need more open, fine sand.

The holes of burrowing wasps can be seen honeycombing the cliffs and other exposed surfaces. The holes are often in 'colonies' although the wasps are themselves solitary. The nest does not have a hierarchy of queen and workers. Instead each mother collects her own food and the visitor may sometimes be able to watch a wasp dragging a caterpillar or other prey back to her nest to provide a larder for the grubs that hatch from her eggs. These burrowing wasps are more slender than the familiar common wasp, and not all have yellow and black stripes.

Solitary mining bees may also be seen, many of which look like small honey bees. (Many types of insect emerge fully grown from the pupal stage – a small fly or bee is never a youngster but of a different species.)

There are also some rare and localised beetles. Although few might wish to handle a live beetle, they do attract their own devotees. At the turn of the century some clerics were quizzing an eminent biologist on his view of God. 'He has an inordinate fondness for beetles,' came his considered reply. Indeed, there are thousands of different species of beetle to be found in Britain, in almost every habitat.

There are many attractive wild flowers including viper's-bugloss (flowering 6–9). Evening primrose (6–9) can also be seen – its large flowers open at dusk to be visited by night-flying moths which pollinate them.

Management
Many problems have arisen in the past due to illegal motor bike scrambling and, to a lesser extent, horse riding. Both activities have been reduced by the erection of a fence. Some scrub has been cleared from the bottom of the pit.

The Cothill Reserves **Hitchcopse Pit**

OS sheet 164; SU 452996

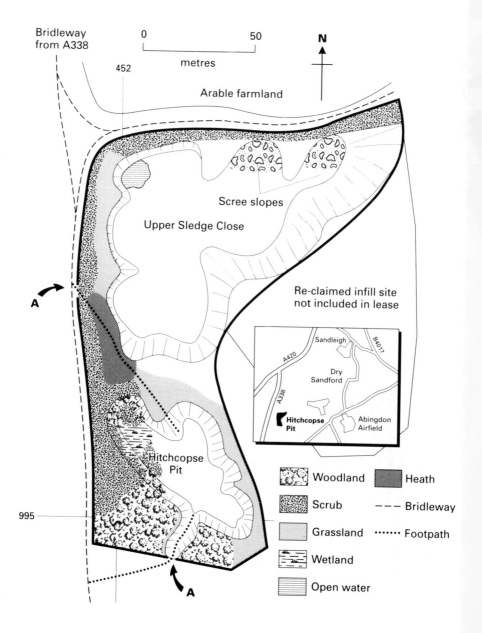

Bridleway from A338

Arable farmland

0 — 50
metres

N

452

Scree slopes

Upper Sledge Close

A

Re-claimed infill site
not included in lease

Hitchcopse
Pit

995

A420

Sandleigh

B4017

Dry
Sandford

A338

Hitchcopse
Pit

Abingdon
Airfield

Woodland	Heath
Scrub	--- Bridleway
Grassland	······· Footpath
Wetland	
Open water	

A

Lashford Lane Fen
OS sheet 164; SP 468011

Nearest towns Oxford and Abingdon

A 7 hectare (17.4 acre) wetland SSSI, bought by BBONT in two lots, in 1984 and 1985.

Location
Leave Oxford westwards on the A420 (Botley Road). Go 1½ miles past Cumnor and take the first turning to the left on the unclassified road leading to Abingdon. Take the first turning to the right into Lashford Lane and the reserve is on your right. Park just inside the gate to the reserve.

Access
Open to the public. No dogs.

Description
This is a small wetland site in a valley cutting down into limestone. The seepage of limey water has created soil conditions suitable for plant-rich valley fen. The fen is one of a mosaic of different habitats, others being woodlands of ash and sycamore, willow and birch, hawthorn and other scrub, and areas of flower-rich grassland. Sandford Brook runs through the site.

Rich fen such as we have here – nationally an exceptionally scarce habitat – is to be prized. The plants which set the scene are tall reed and lushly growing great willowherb (flowering 7–8), meadowsweet (6–9) and hemp-agrimony (7–9). Amongst these grow slighter plants, many with attractive flowers, including creeping-Jenny (6–8). In the centre of the fen is a rather more acidic area which is marked by purple moor-grass.

Smooth newts are living in the centre of the fen. Great crested newts may be present too. These are now nationally rare, so much so that they are one of a number of protected species that it is illegal to kill or disturb. Today's countryside is generally too hostile for these newts and they rely on refuges such as this nature reserve. Protected as they are, in the open countryside they may still be harmed by 'lawful activities' – which include agricultural practice. This one example is enough to show just how important nature reserves are, and how vital BBONT's work is, if we want to protect wildlife.

There are three areas of limestone grassland on the reserve where visitors may see many wild flowers such as dwarf thistle (flowering 6–9), fairy flax (6–9) and burnet-saxifrage (7–8).

The scrub and reeds attract many breeding warblers and other songbirds while the marbled white butterfly is one of many insects and other invertebrates for which the reserve is renowned.

Management
Scrub clearance is needed and the grassland areas need mowing and/or grazing to keep them open. Trees in the fen areas are removed and the reed beds cut on a rotational basis.

The Cothill Reserves **Lashford Lane Fen**

OS sheet 164; SP 468011

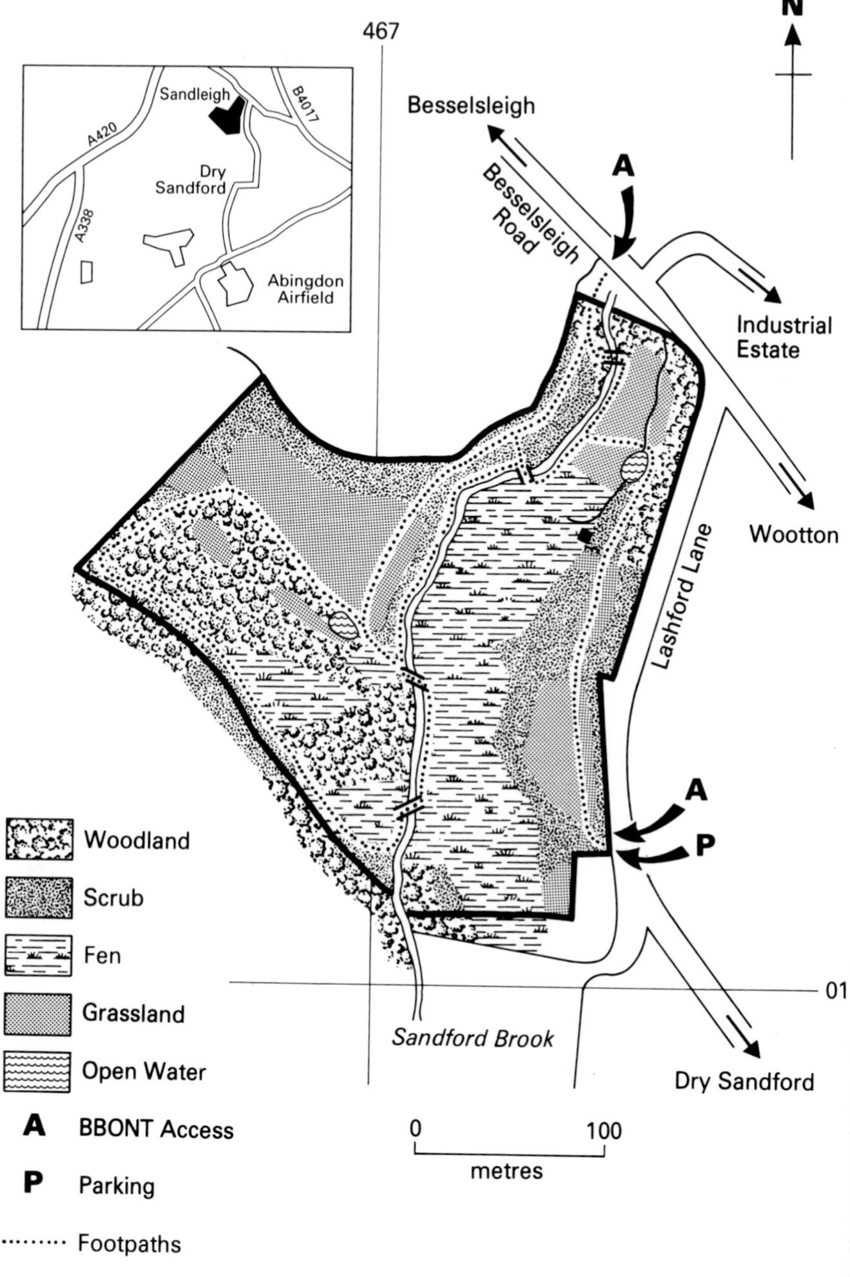

N

467

Besselsleigh

Sandleigh

B4017

A420

Dry Sandford

A338

Abingdon Airfield

Besselsleigh Road

A

Industrial Estate

Wootton

Lashford Lane

A

P

01

Woodland

Scrub

Fen

Grassland

Open Water

A BBONT Access

P Parking

········· Footpaths

Sandford Brook

Dry Sandford

0 ____ 100

metres

Parsonage Moor

OS sheet 164; SU 462998

Nearest towns Abingdon and Oxford

The 12 hectare (30 acre) reserve is part of the Cothill Fen SSSI. BBONT manages it by separate agreements, dated 1980 and 1981, with the two owners.

Location

Park in the car park for DRY SANDFORD PIT reserve (see page 38 for directions). Walk back to the road, and turn left, walking along the road until you reach the Merry Miller restaurant. Take the footpath leading from the far corner of the car park on the opposite side of the road from the restaurant, and follow this for about 300 metres. You will see the gate and signboard for Parsonage Moor on your right, just before a stile.

Access

Only the paths are open the public. Do not step off the paths as the fen is dangerously deep in places.

Description

This is part of the 22 hectare Cothill Fen SSSI, one of the best fenland sites in the county. It has outstanding, and now nationally rare, calcareous (limey) fen as well as other wetland habitats. Altogether the SSSI shows succession from open water to fen and carr (wet woodland) with an nearby area of ancient woodland.

Over 300 different plant species have been recorded on the SSSI – a very large number in relation to its size. Unusually, both 'lime-liking' and 'lime-hating' species can be seen. This is the result of the complex soil profile of the area, which has grits covered by peat and marl and fed by rather limey water.

BBONT's reserve encompasses most of the open fenland and extensive reedbeds and also includes some scrub and woodland. There are many wild flowers to interest visitors, such as grass-of-Parnassus (flowering 7–10), common butterwort (5–7), round-leaved sundew (6–8), dyer's greenweed (6–10) and both narrow-leaved (5–6) and southern (6–8) marsh-orchid.

Being so close to Oxford, this interesting place has a long history of research. A long-term study on the population dynamics and genetics of the scarlet tiger moth has become famous. The reserve is very rich in moths and dragonflies. It is also a particularly good place for birds, especially winter migrants.

Management

Cothill Fen is a National Nature Reserve managed by English Nature. Parsonage Moor itself is suffering from the invasion of scrub of various kinds and this is being removed.

It is hoped that a part of the fen area can be excavated with the intention of studying the succession from open water back to fen.

The Cothill Reserves
Parsonage Moor
OS sheet 164; SU 462998

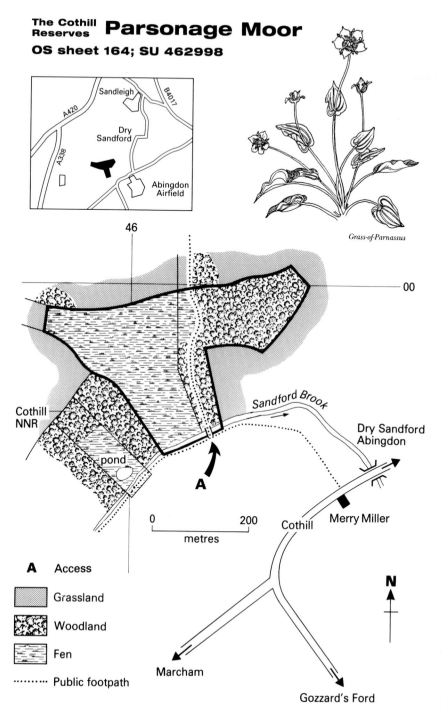

Grass-of-Parnassus

A   Access

Grassland

Woodland

Fen

.... Public footpath

Dancersend & The Crong Meadow

OS sheet 165; SP 900095 (Dancersend), SP 904088 (The Crong Meadow)

Nearest towns Wendover and Tring

Thirty-three hectares (81.6 acres) in all, made up of 30 hectares (73 acres) of woodland, 2 hectares (6 acres) of grassland and scrub, and the additional 1 hectare (2.6 acres) of the Crong Meadow. The Dancersend reserve is owned by the Royal Society for Nature Conservation, and leased to BBONT and the Forestry Commission. The whole reserve is part of a larger SSSI. The Crong Meadow has been held since 1987 on a 50 year lease from Thames Water.

Location

From Wendover take the A4011 towards Tring and turn sharp right just before the A41 onto the unclassified road to St Leonards. After 1½ miles there is a sharp left-hand bend by a pond. Park on the right-hand verge, opposite the pond, or in the pull-in on the left, and walk up the track opposite the bend to Dancersend reserve. For the Crong Meadow, continue along the unclassified road for another mile, until you reach the waterworks buildings on the left. Park in the yard at the back, making sure that you do not block the gates or garages. The meadow is on the opposite side of the road.

Access

Open to the public along footpaths and trails, as shown on the map (see page 49). Dogs are not allowed in the Crong Meadow when stock are grazing.

Description

Dancersend reserve includes a range of Chiltern habitats on the slopes of two dry valleys, rising to an altitude of 255 metres, only 12 metres short of the highest point in the Chilterns. The soil varies, being quite acidic in the higher woodland and alkaline in the lower grassland areas. Differences in soil, aspect and management have produced favourable conditions for a rich variety of wildlife, including rare moths and butterflies and over 290 different plants.

Most of the woodlands used to be beech with some oak, but these were felled during World War II, and left to be colonised by scrub. In the mid 1950s, most of the area was replanted by the Forestry Commission with beech, using larch and spruce as protective cover for the saplings. The rest was allowed to grow with self-sown trees, mainly ash. The conifers are now gradually being removed to reveal a remarkable number of survivors from the original woodland, such as wood vetch (flowering 6–8), stinking hellebore (1–4), and Solomon's-seal (5–6). There are also interesting fungi in autumn, including the earth-star. Such a large area of woodland provides cover for a good many animals, including foxes, muntjac and roe deer, and the fat or edible dormouse, introduced as a novelty into Tring Park in 1902 and now found in various parts of the Chilterns.

The woodlands are home to a variety of birds, including nuthatches, and green and greater spotted woodpeckers. Woodpeckers usually nest in dead trees, and feed on insect caterpillars and grubs which feed in the dead wood. It is only

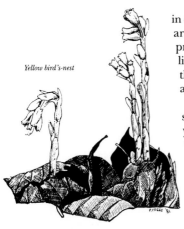

Yellow bird's-nest

in established woodland that enough mature trees are found to support woodpeckers, and their presence here is encouraging. Tawny owls also live in the wood. They are difficult to see, but their 'tu-wit, tu-woo' hooting calls can be heard at dusk.

The central 5 hectares of Dancersend, shown as open grassland on maps of over 100 years ago, have developed into a mixed woodland and scrub, very rich in plants, including the yellow bird's-nest (6–8). This unusual plant does not gain any energy from the sun, so it is not green like most plants. Instead, it gains nourishment from decaying leaf-litter and vegetable matter. Since it has no need of sunlight, it can grow in the dense shade of beechwoods where other plants cannot survive.

The scrub areas are cut in rotation, providing a continuous supply of sheltered clearings. The clearings encourage rare butterflies such as the grizzled skipper and Duke of Burgundy. The Duke of Burgundy is becoming very scarce in Britain. Its caterpillars feed on primrose and cowslip, and need strongly-growing lush plants which will not dry out during the summer. Such plants grow best in new clearings, where the fairly bare ground is warm and sheltered enough for them to do well. However, after a few years other more vigorous plants will over-shadow the primroses and cowslips, making them unsuitable for Duke of Burgundy caterpillars. For this reason, it is essential that new clearings are always available for the plants and butterflies to re-colonise.

The jewel of Dancersend reserve is a small area of chalk grassland saved from complete scrub invasion. This area has been the subject of research into reclaiming chalk grassland from over-grown scrub. In the 1960s, the Hon. Miriam Rothschild carried out experiments on maintaining grassland by small-scale sheep-grazing, and in the 1980s Clive Turner tried out different methods of cutting back dogwood to prevent it taking the grassland over. These research programmes produced much useful information, which has since been applied to the management of BBONT's other grassland reserves.

This grassland area of Dancersend now has pyramidal, fragrant and bee orchids (at their best in June), common spotted-orchids (6–7), Chiltern gentian (8–9) and many butterflies including the green hairstreak and dark green fritillary.

Duke of Burgundy

47

Adder's-tongue

The Crong Meadow, adjacent to Dancersend reserve, provides another area of 'unimproved' chalk grassland – i.e. grassland which has not been ploughed for many years, if ever. The grassland has also escaped spraying with herbicides or feeding with artificial fertilizers. It was sold to Thames Water in the 1940s, and since then it has been grazed intermittently by horses or beef cattle.

The fact that it has not been ploughed or improved means that it contains a large variety of wild flowers and other plants – over 130 have so far been recorded, including adder's-tongue and cuckooflower, normally found in wetter meadows than this. Many of the plants here are food and nectar sources for a range of butterflies including marbled white, ringlet and meadow brown. There are also sightings of the white admiral butterfly, a woodland species with a liking for sunny glades. Presumably it comes from the woods of the Dancersend reserve to gain nectar from the grassland flowers.

Haphazard grazing regimes in the past have resulted in the invasion of hawthorn and other scrub species onto the open ground. Today's management of the reserve includes carefully planned grazing to allow the distinctive plants to grow. Undergrazing would allow scrub to invade the area. Overgrazing might control the scrub but could also wipe out colonies of flowers. Grazing at the wrong time of year (before the plants produce seeds) might endanger some species of wild flowers in the long term (and it might also jeopardise the survival of the many butterflies and other invertebrates which depend on them).

The livestock used for the grazing is also important as they feed in rather different ways. Cattle and horses tear at the grass. If the heavier horses and cattle graze when the ground is soft after heavy rain, there is danger that it will be 'poached', churned to mud. Sheep graze closely to produce a fine low sward.

Management

In Dancersend reserve, blocks of woodland are being thinned or coppiced and clearings created. Rides through the wood are kept open, and an area of scrub is being cut on a short rotation. The meadow plots are kept free of invading scrub, and different heights of vegetation are obtained by a mixture of mowing and sheep grazing.

The BBONT sheep flock also graze the Crong Meadow as part of a carefully managed grazing regime. Scrub needs to be cut on a rotation system, so that there is enough left to provide shelter for birds and butterflies without crowding out the smaller grassland plants.

Dancersend & The Crong Meadow

OS sheet 165; SP 900095 (Dancersend), SP 904088 (The Crong Meadow)

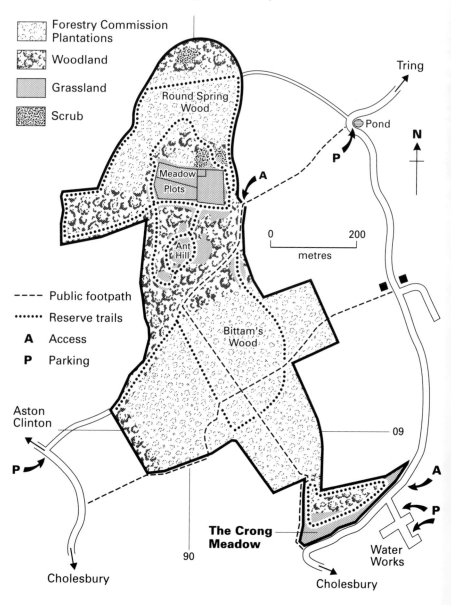

Forestry Commission Plantations

Woodland

Grassland

Scrub

Round Spring Wood

Tring

Pond

P

N

Meadow Plots

A

0   200
metres

Ant Hill

- - - Public footpath
········ Reserve trails
A Access
P Parking

Bittam's Wood

Aston Clinton

P

09

A

P

The Crong Meadow

90

Water Works

Cholesbury

Cholesbury

49

Decoy Heath

OS sheet; 175; SU 615635

Nearest town Reading

Decoy Heath is a 7 hectare (17 acre) reserve which is part of a larger SSSI. Previously a gravel extraction site, it has regenerated naturally since it was infilled in the early 1980s. In 1993, BBONT signed a 50 year lease from John Stacey and Sons Ltd for the site.

Location
At junction 12 of the M4 take the A4 towards Newbury. Turn left onto the A340 to Aldermaston. Drive through Aldermaston village and take the left fork signposted to Silchester. Follow the road for about 2 miles and at the T-junction turn right and take the Silchester exit at the Valentine Wood roundabout. The car park is 200 metres on the right, opposite the entrance to a factory.

Access
Open to the public.

Description
The reserve consists of a range of habitats, including heath, woodland and areas of open water. This is the richest site for dragonflies and damselflies in Berkshire, with 23 species known to breed around the shallow pools of the reserve. These include the nationally rare downy emerald and brilliant emerald dragonflies, and the scarce blue-tailed damselfly. The latter breeds in newly created shallow pools, and this is its only known site in Berkshire. The dragonflies hunt insects over the pools and valley bog. The insects are attracted to flowers which include yellow iris (6–8), marsh speedwell (6–8), lesser skullcap (6–8) and marsh violet (4–7). The pools also contain various rushes and sedges, providing cover for nesting mallards, moorhens, lapwings and little ringed plovers.

The more open area of heath has characteristic species such as ling (7–9) and smaller amounts of bell heather (5–9), common gorse (all year) and broom (4–6). Grass snakes and adders can often be found basking in the sunshine. The heath is edged by small areas with plants typical of wastelands, such as nettles (6–9), oxeye daisy (5–9), red bartsia (6–9) and perforate St John's-wort (7–9).

Just under half the reserve is covered by young semi-natural woodland consisting mainly of silver birch and Scots pine, interspersed by oak, rowan and wild cherry among others. The woodland provides cover and breeding sites for many birds such as the green woodpecker, nuthatch, tawny owl and linnet. Other birds are regular visitors, with siskins and redpolls feeding on the alders at the southern boundary of the reserve. In total, at least 82 bird species frequent the reserve. The woodland also supports wild flowers, such as honeysuckle (6–10), foxglove (6–9), early forget-me-not (4–6) and primrose (3–5). Wild flowers on the heath attract grayling, Essex skipper and silver-studded blue butterflies.

Management
The heathland requires grazing and scrub removal to maintain and restore it. New shallow pools are created periodically to provide suitable habitat for dragonflies.

Decoy Heath

OS sheet; 175; SU 615635

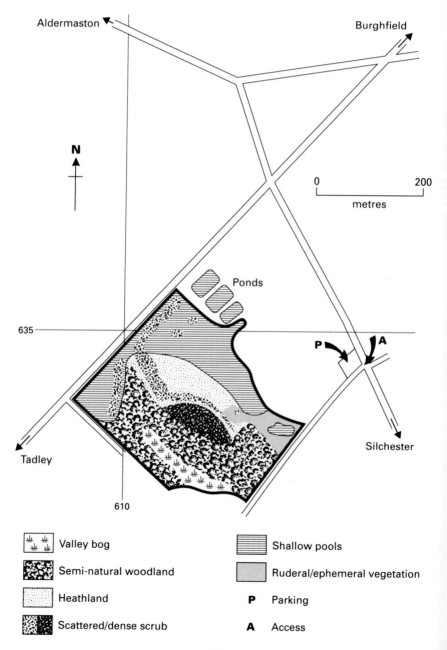

Aldermaston

Burghfield

N

0 — 200
metres

Ponds

635

P

A

610

Tadley

Silchester

	Valley bog		Shallow pools
	Semi-natural woodland		Ruderal/ephemeral vegetation
	Heathland	**P**	Parking
	Scattered/dense scrub	**A**	Access

51

Finemere Wood
OS Sheet 165; SP 721215

Nearest town Winslow

An ancient woodland of 40.3 hectares (109 acres), bought by BBONT in 1989. With some adjoining grassland and scrub it was designated an SSSI in 1990.

Location

The wood lies to the north of the road between Quainton and Edgcott (which lies north of the A41 between Aylesbury and Bicester). Travelling west from Quainton, turn left at a T-junction, signposted to Edgcott. After about ¾ mile, a graded track leaves the road to the right. Park on the verge nearby. The track leads to the wood entrance, for which the grid reference is given above. There is a circular wildlife walk and other permissive paths in the wood.

Access
Open to the public.

Description
The wood was originally part of the Great Forest of Bernwood but was then cleared and replanted during the 1950s and 1960s. A central area has now been cleared where a historic meadow once divided the woodland. Many old meadow species still remain. Two streams run through the wood into the adjoining River Ray, which winds its way to Otmoor, Oxfordshire.

As a result of the variation in moisture and mineral content of the soil and the chequered management history of the wood, a rich mosaic of habitats may be found. Some 200 hundred species of flowering plant have been recorded, including yellow archangel (flowering 5–6), bluebell (4–6) and sweet woodruff (5–6). Habitats include plantations of Scots pine and Norway spruce (our 'Christmas' tree). Compartments where replanting failed vary from dwarf conifers to mixed scrub and the occasional oak standard. There are fragments of the original woodland, which have been unmanaged for many decades. In these the 'coppice with standards' management system has developed into a high forest of overgrown oak over hazel coppice, with blackthorn brakes and aspen groves marking the damper areas. Giant ancient ash and maple coppice stools survive on the drier, north-western reaches of the wood.

The wood is exceptional for butterflies, with the nationally rare wood white and black hairstreak figuring amongst over 20 recorded species. Breeding birds include nightingale, woodcock, goldcrest and all three British woodpeckers. Grass snakes and common lizards bask in the sunny rides and glades. Foxes and muntjac deer are often seen.

Management
The main conifer plantings have been thinned, with rides being widened and scalloped to benefit butterflies and birds. Coppicing has been reintroduced on various rotations to create a structure attractive to nightingales and warblers. Interpretative boards have been placed at the reserve to explain some of these management practices.

Finemere Wood

OS Sheet 165; SP 721215

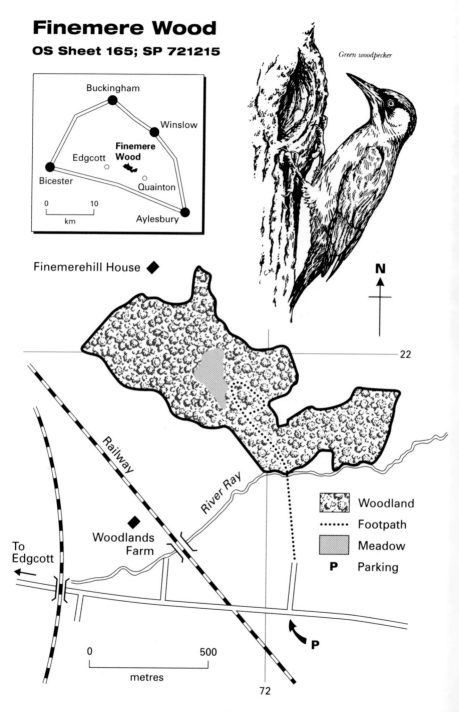

Green woodpecker

Buckingham

Winslow

Edgcott **Finemere Wood**

Bicester Quainton

Aylesbury

0 10
km

Finemerehill House ◆

N

22

Railway

River Ray

To
Edgcott

Woodlands
Farm

🔲 Woodland
······ Footpath
🔲 Meadow
P Parking

0 500
metres

P

72

Foxholes

OS sheet 163; SP 254206

Nearest towns Burford and Chipping Norton

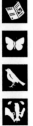

A reserve of 64 hectares (158 acres) encompassing a variety of habitats, including a wet meadow. Much of the reserve is of SSSI status. Part of it is owned by BBONT and part has been leased since 1975 on a 99 year lease.

Location

From Burford take the A424 towards Stow-on-the-Wold. Take the third lane on the right and just before Bruern Abbey turn left along a rough track following the western edge of Cocksmoor Wood. After ½ mile, the car park is reached, on the right at SP 259208. Cars are taken down the track at the owners' risk.

Access

The public footpaths and bridleways are open to the public. The waymarked route is open to BBONT members only.

Description

Foxholes Reserve, together with surrounding woodland, is known by local people as 'Bould Wood'. The woodland is a remnant of the ancient Wychwood Forest, sloping gently from higher ground with acidic soil, across base-rich (alkaline) soils, down to the River Evenlode. Soil and management over the centuries have combined to create a variety of habitats. For example, in the part of the reserve next to Cocksmoor Wood two kinds of wet ash and maple woodland can be recognised. Both have coppiced trees, shrubs and wild flowers. However, in one, flowering plants include primrose (3–6) together with early-purple orchid (4–6), common twayblade (6–7), and wild angelica (6–9), while the other (where oak and ash standard trees are seen) has plants not common elsewhere in the wood, including sanicle (5–8), goldilocks buttercup (4–6) and herb-Paris (5–7).

Elsewhere in the reserve there are a few mature oaks. Beeches, hornbeams and larches have been planted. The Bruern estate (from which BBONT leases part of the reserve) has thinned the beechwood area in Ladies Ride and replanted with a mixture of mainly deciduous trees.

The woodland is excellent for fungi. In the open rides on acidic soils, plants such as purple moor-grass, bog moss and heath spotted-orchid (flowering 6–8) can be seen. Uncommon mosses and liverworts are also found. In the wet meadow alongside the river, great burnet (5–8) and devil's-bit scabious (6–10) flower.

Over 20 species of butterfly have been recorded, including the rare wood white. Muntjac, fallow deer and foxes use the reserve, and both the grass snake and adder are common, although the latter is now in decline. The bird life is abundant and varied.

Management

The rides must be maintained and horse barriers repaired. Some old ash coppice is being re-coppiced. The meadow is grazed and the newly planted willow is protected. Ponds and nestboxes are maintained. There is a new 1 hectare plantation in Roughborough Copse, 70% of which is oak and the remainder cherry, rowan and ash.

Foxholes

OS sheet 163; SP 254206

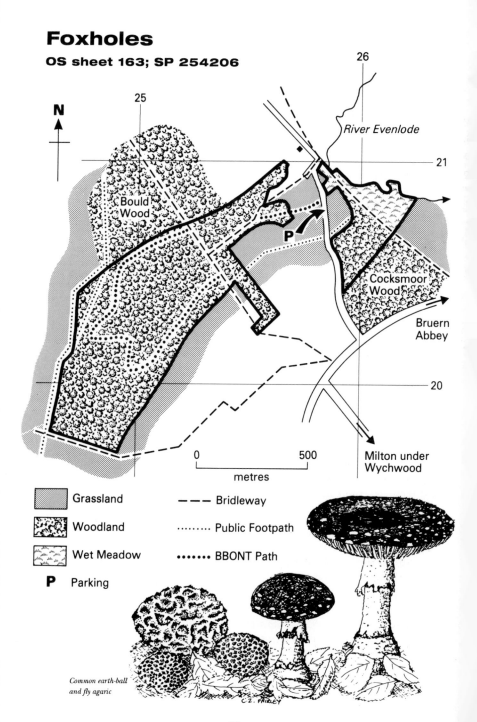

River Evenlode

Bould Wood

P

Cocksmoor Wood

Bruern Abbey

Milton under Wychwood

0 — 500
metres

Grassland
Woodland
Wet Meadow
P Parking

– – – Bridleway
.... Public Footpath
•••••• BBONT Path

*Common earth-ball
and fly agaric*

55

Grangelands

OS sheet 165; SP 827049

Nearest town Princes Risborough

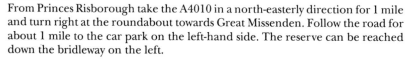

An 11 hectare (27 acre) area of chalk grassland with some scrub, overlooked by woodland on Pulpit Hill. BBONT manages part of the Grangelands site by agreement with Buckinghamshire County Council. Pulpit Hill belongs to the National Trust.

Location

From Princes Risborough take the A4010 in a north-easterly direction for 1 mile and turn right at the roundabout towards Great Missenden. Follow the road for about 1 mile to the car park on the left-hand side. The reserve can be reached down the bridleway on the left.

Access

Grangelands, including the disused rifle range, is open to the public. Please note that some of Pulpit Hill is very steep and impenetrable where thickly overgrown with scrub.

Description

Pulpit Hill is basically beech woodland with whitebeams and yew. The path leads down the hill, opening up on the left to show views of the Vale of Aylesbury and the grassland of Grangelands. This ancient, flowery chalk sward was ploughed up during World War II, reverted to grassland, and since then has recovered remarkably well. It has been recolonized and there is now a good display of plants and butterflies to be seen. Juniper, a rare shrub in Britain, is also successfully regenerating.

The marbled white is one of the butterflies found here. On the wing in July and August, the female, unusually among butterflies, drops her eggs casually amongst the grass. She makes no attempt to attach them to the grass stems or leaf blades on which the caterpillars will feed. Whereas other newly-hatched and hungry caterpillars would be at a disadvantage, those of the marbled white eat their egg case and then retire soon afterwards to hibernate deep within a grass tussock, waking on warm days after the turn of the year to feed on the fresh growth. The seemingly haphazard actions of wildlife – the things that might be found puzzling on a walk – often have an explanation once the whole story is known.

On this reserve, the chalkhill blue butterfly has also been studied, as have glow-worms and various bumble bees.

Management

The grassland has been fenced and is now being grazed. Scrub control is needed, especially at the bottom of Pulpit Hill. However, areas of scrub in the valley bottoms are being retained to provide shelter and nesting sites for birds. On Pulpit Hill itself, over-mature beech trees have been felled and replanted.

Grangelands

OS sheet 165; SP 827049

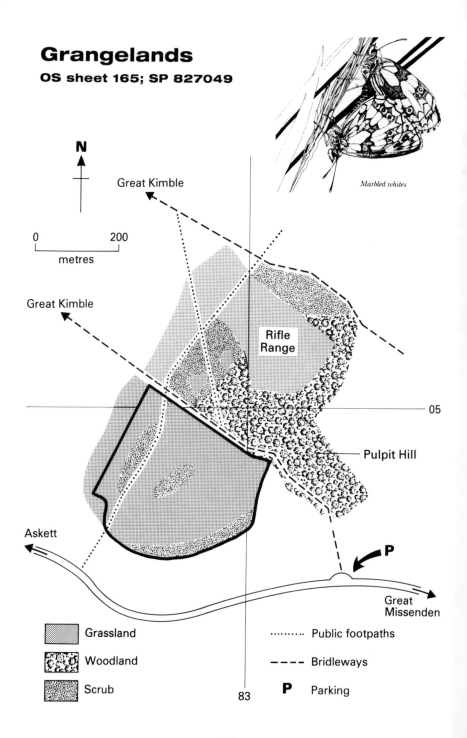

Marbled whites

N

0   200

metres

Great Kimble

Great Kimble

Rifle Range

Pulpit Hill

05

Askett

P

Great Missenden

83

	Grassland		··········	Public footpaths
	Woodland		– – –	Bridleways
	Scrub		**P**	Parking

Henry Stephen/C.S. Lewis Reserve
OS sheet 164; SP 560065

Nearest town Oxford

A large man-made pond surrounded by a mixed woodland, 3 hectares (7½ acres) in area. The freehold was bought by BBONT in 1969. The reserve is named after C.S. Lewis, an Oxford figure of some renown (and author of the classic children's book *The Lion, the Witch and the Wardrobe* amongst others), and Henry Stephen, a professor of the University, who lived in Lewis Close.

Location
From the Headington roundabout on the A40 north-east of Oxford go south on the ring road, take the first turn on the left and then go immediately right into Kiln Lane. Lewis Close is the fourth turning (about 300 metres) on the right. Park at the end of the close. The reserve is at the end of the path.

Access
Open to the public.

Description
The site was once owned by author C.S. Lewis, a friend of J.R.R. Tolkien. It is said that the worlds of Narnia and Middle Earth (Tolkien's famous hobbit territory) were dreamed up here. So the site might well be a memorial to the imagination as well as being of great wildlife interest.

The large pond was created during the last century when clay was dug. This pond is deep and muddy and under no circumstances should visitors wade into it. It is full of aquatic plants. Many toads migrate here to spawn in spring. The spectacular displays of damselflies and dragonflies alone are worth a visit in summer months. Moorhens and coots regularly nest here. A small stream flows in from the east, and giant horsetail grows at its silty margins.

On the wooded slopes above, beech, oak, birch, alder, sycamore and larch can be seen. Numerous woodland birds are to be heard in spring and early summer, and the scuttlings of small mammals at any time of year. A path leads past the 'doggers': these are large, rounded, sandstone boulders littered on the slopes amid the trees. At the top of the slope is a group of horse chestnuts, and further on an area replanted with native trees.

The reserve is used regularly by school parties for pond dipping and a variety of environmental projects. There is a field study hut for school parties.

Management
The invasive sycamores are removed and 'habitat piles' are created from felled trees and brushwood – the rotting wood will attract a host of beetles and other invertebrate life. Unstable larches at the top of the reserve are being removed and young oak, rowan and a few beech trees are being planted. The pond will be dredged, and the overhanging trees will be cut back to reduce shading. Glades will be created for basking butterflies. A new bat hibernaculum will, it is hoped, provide winter quarters for local bats.

Henry Stephen/C.S. Lewis Reserve

OS sheet 164; SP 560065

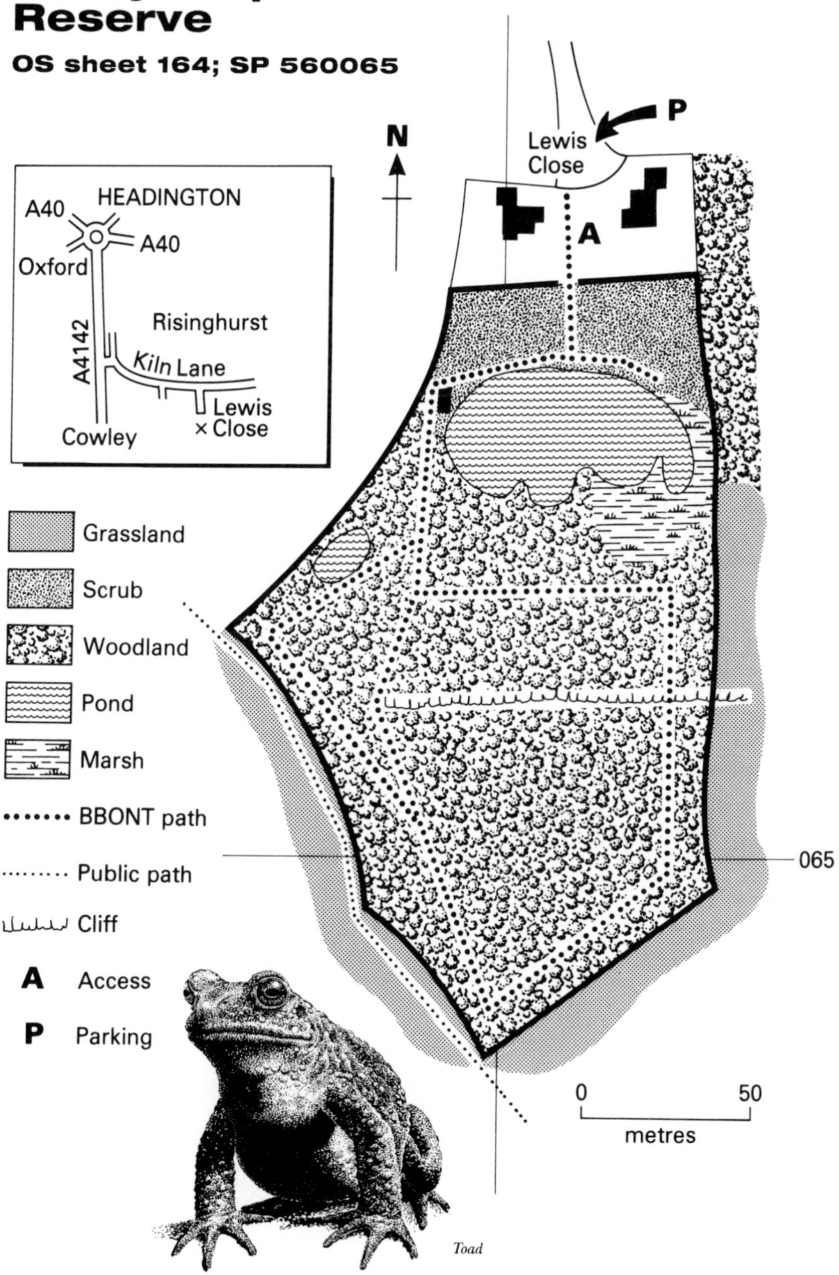

N

Lewis Close

P

A

HEADINGTON

A40

A40

Oxford

A4142

Risinghurst

Kiln Lane

Lewis × Close

Cowley

Grassland

Scrub

Woodland

Pond

Marsh

•••••• BBONT path

········ Public path

⌣⌣⌣⌣ Cliff

A   Access

P   Parking

065

0   50
metres

Toad

Inkpen Common

OS sheet 174; SU 382643

Nearest town Hungerford

Heathland (with bog) and areas of woodland, 10.4 hectares (26 acres) in extent. An SSSI, owned by BBONT.

Location

Leave the A4 3½ miles east of Hungerford, on the road leading south to Kintbury. Take the second turn to the left in Kintbury village, following the road to East and West Woodhay for about 1¼ miles. Bear right at Rooksnest Farm, signposted Inkpen Common. The main part of the reserve is on the left opposite a row of small houses. Cars may be parked on the verge on the left, at the corner of Heads Lane and the bridleway to Foxhills.

Access

Open to the public. Horse riding is restricted to the bridleway along the south-east boundary of the reserve.

Description

Here, the acidic soil encourages heathland plants. The reserve is a remnant of the former Inkpen Great Common, and in the past it was kept clear of gorse bushes, birch and other trees because the local people had rights on common land to graze their livestock, collect firewood, heather and bracken (for bedding) and gorse (for firing bread ovens).

The reserve is in two parts. The smaller south-western area is now a small wood of naturally regenerated oak and birch on an abandoned area of heath. In the larger eastern part an area of damp heathland survives, a 'wilderness' of a kind now scarce in Berkshire. Even here there are patches of woodland growing at the expense of the heather and gorse. Although in full heavy scented bloom in spring, common gorse always bears a flower or two ("when gorse is out of bloom, kissing is out of fashion", as they used to say). Dwarf gorse, with softer spines than its relative, is also present (flowering 7–9).

The heathland has purple moor-grass (in flower rather late in the year, 8–9), heather (7–10), bell heather (7–9) and cross-leaved heath (6–9). The heathers can be distinguished not only by the arrangement of their small leaves, but by the fact that the first two occupy drier ground, and the third wetter ground. Lousewort (4–7) flowers abundantly in places, and the uncommon pale dog-violet can be seen (5–6).

The reserve includes a small valley bog, fed by water seepage. The most dramatic flower here is bog asphodel with glorious yellow flowers (7–8). It is equally striking later, when both seed pods and leaves become orange. Meadow thistle (6–7) and petty whin (4–7) also mark parts of this wetter area.

Not only important for its heath, the reserve is populated by many summer nesting birds.

Management

The invasive gorse and birch need to be controlled to allow the heathers to flourish. Coppicing creates suitable sites for nesting birds.

Inkpen Common

OS sheet 174; SU 382643

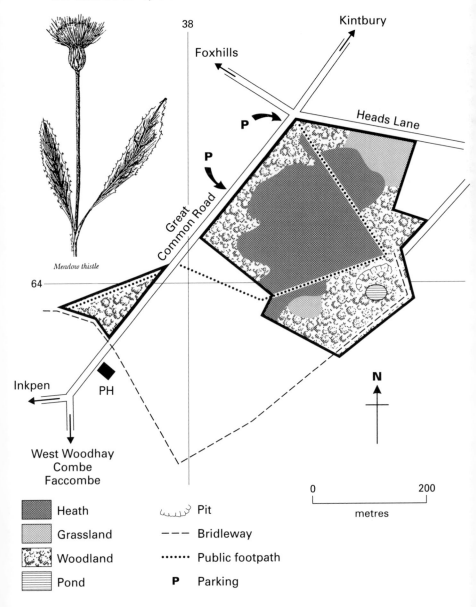

Kintbury

Foxhills

Heads Lane

P

P

Great Common Road

Meadow thistle

Inkpen

PH

West Woodhay
Combe
Faccombe

N

0   200

metres

Heath	Pit
Grassland	– – – Bridleway
Woodland	•••••• Public footpath
Pond	**P** Parking

Little Linford Wood

OS sheet 152; SP 834455

Nearest towns Milton Keynes and Newport Pagnell

An ancient woodland of 42.5 hectares (105 acres), with some felled areas which have been replanted. It has been owned by BBONT since 1986.

Location

From Newport Pagnell take the B526 north. Just before Gayhurst turn left towards Haversham. After ½ mile turn right through a farm gate marked Dairy Farm and follow the rough track under the M1 motorway, past Dairy Farm to the car park at Little Linford Wood.

Access

Open to the public on foot along all rides and bridleways. Swan's Way, a long distance bridleway from Salcey Forest to Goring-on-Thames, runs through the wood. Horses must keep to the bridleways. Dogs must be kept on leads.

Description

This ancient woodland is marked on a map dated 1766 and so it is likely that it has never been cleared for agriculture. From medieval times and often much earlier, these old woodlands were being managed without much replanting, the villagers exploiting the fact that trees do not have a fixed life span. Trees and shrubs were regularly coppiced, cut down to almost ground level and allow to grow back. This gave a reliable supply of small wood. Certain saplings were left (or planted) as 'standards' to grow tall, eventually being felled, each in their prime, for timber. The woodland must always have been rich in spring flowers but especially where the trees were coppiced. This opened the woodland floor to light, encouraging bluebells (4–6) and other flowers.

The recent history of Little Linford Wood is less pleasant. About 100 years ago, the wood was felled and replanted. Just before it passed into BBONT's care, about a third of the area was completely felled, with 70 or 80 mature oaks also removed from the northern area. However, coppice regrowth is taking place and, with some replanting of new trees, the wood will recover in due course.

The principal trees are oak, ash and field maple, and there is also some wild cherry. Sycamore is present but needs to be controlled. So far about 130 different species of flowering shrubs, woodland flowers and other plants have been recorded, including 23 found only in ancient woodland, an example of which is the local herb-Paris (flowering 5–6).

Management

A great deal of work has already been carried out but much remains to be done. Replanting and work on the rides were carried out during 1987/88. The open rides will be managed to create conditions suitable for a wide range of species and to act as routes for timber extraction. A car park and new pond have been created at the entrance with a circular nature trail. The woodland is traditionally managed by coppicing to produce sustainable woodland products, such as charcoal and hurdles, during the winter.

Little Linford Wood

OS sheet 152; SP 834455

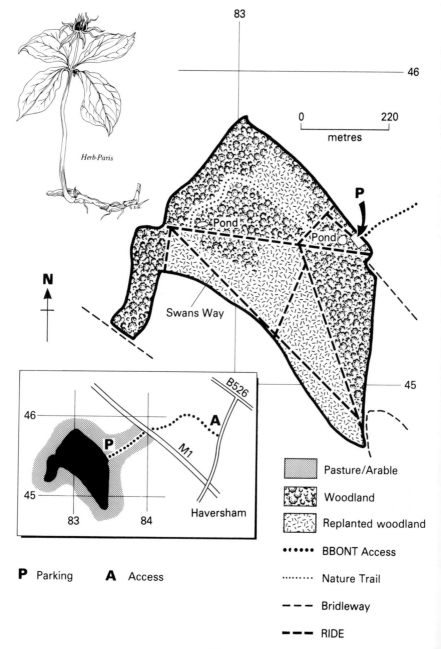

Herb-Paris

83

46

0   220
metres

P

Pond

Pond

N

Swans Way

B526

46

A

P

M1

45

83   84   Haversham

45

	Pasture/Arable
	Woodland
	Replanted woodland

••••• BBONT Access

········· Nature Trail

– – – Bridleway

━ ━ ━ RIDE

P Parking   **A** Access

Loddon Reserve

OS sheet 175; SU 785758

Nearest town Twyford

One of the largest of a group of flooded gravel pits, approximately 13.8 hectares (34 acres) in extent. The open water is surrounded by a strip of scrub. BBONT leases the reserve from the gravel extraction company.

Location

The reserve lies south of the Old Bath Road on the edge of Twyford. Park in the public car park in Polehampton Lane. To reach the reserve, walk west along the main road past the railway, until just before the factory (old mill site), and take a signposted footpath which leaves on the left. This crosses the River Loddon by a footbridge and the path (often muddy and slippery) continues southwards to reach a pool and sluice. Cross the sluice and continue. The reserve boundary is reached where the path turns sharp right. The footpath can then be followed within the reserve.

Access

Open to the public on the length of footpath described above. There is a path around the whole of the lake. To avoid disturbing the birds, please do not go too close to the lake edge and do keep dogs away from the water.

Description

The River Loddon takes numerous channels around Twyford, branching and rejoining. Another main channel runs down the western side of the reserve. This 'braiding' is the normal and natural behaviour of a river, but river engineering during recent centuries has largely eliminated such random meanders, and has also resulted in the loss of a vast amount of water and waterside habitat.

This reserve, however, is one example of how some of that loss has been made good, gravel diggings having been allowed to flood and revert to nature. The contours of the shallow diggings have created a lake with an attractively scalloped edge, several islands and a surrounding strip of land now covered with scrub. These islands are a bonus for waterfowl, giving some protection from predators such as foxes. As a result, terns and lapwing have nested safely in the past. Herons, coots and great crested grebes are regulars at the reserve. The grebes are particularly noticeable in spring with their remarkable courtship displays. The scrub margin attracts blackcaps, whitethroats and other songbirds. In all, 70 species have been recorded. The reserve is also valued for its dragonflies and damselflies, and 16 species of butterfly have been recorded.

Winter too is a busy time, with a greater variety of waterfowl, including tufted duck, pochard, cormorant and the occasional snipe.

Management

The management of the reserve will aim at maintaining the variety of habitats which has given rise to such high bird and butterfly counts.

Loddon Reserve
OS sheet 175; SU 785758

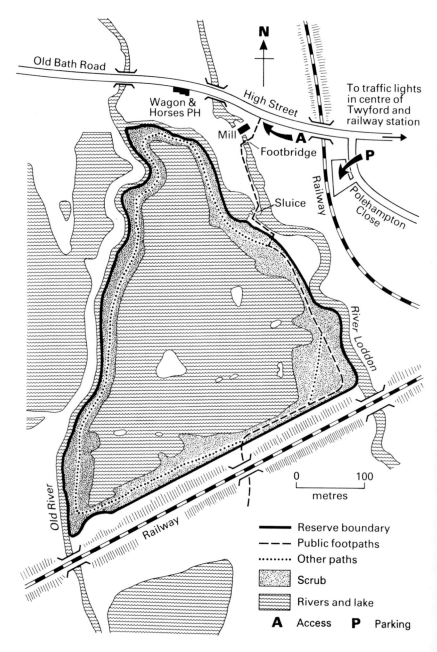

N

Old Bath Road

High Street

Wagon & Horses PH

Mill

Footbridge

Sluice

To traffic lights in centre of Twyford and railway station

P

Railway

Polehampton Close

River Loddon

Old River

Railway

A

0   100
metres

——— Reserve boundary
– – – Public footpaths
········ Other paths
▒ Scrub
〜 Rivers and lake
A Access   **P** Parking

Moor Copse
OS sheet 175; SU 633738

Nearest town Reading

Varied woodland, 26.8 hectares (67 acres) in area and the major part of an SSSI. BBONT was left freehold ownership in 1975 and acquired Bartons Copse in 1988. The length of the River Pang running through the reserve was bought by BBONT in 1975.

Location
Leave Pangbourne southwards on the A340. Just past Tidmarsh, as you rise to cross the M4, turn left into a lay-by with parking. The reserve is on the left.

Access
Open to the public.

Description
The reserve consists of several areas of woodland. Hogmoor Copse, the first area to greet the visitor, is a wet wood on peat and gravel, with willows and a few oak and ash trees. About two-thirds of it was thinned or coppiced in 1990, while the northern third has been left as a non-intervention area. Drainage ditches have been dug across it in the past, the reason for which is not clear.

Park Wood, on the other hand, is a type of ancient landscape very familiar to our ancestors, although not much like film versions of the greenwood. This ancient woodland consists of areas of coppiced alder and hazel, overshadowed by giant single-trunked 'standard' oak trees. The coppicing gives the wood an airy cathedral-like feel, and by opening the woodland floor to light it encourages a breathtaking display of primroses (flowering 3–6) and bluebells (4–6). There is also a small stand of Norway spruce (Christmas trees) in Park Wood.

A 2 hectare hay field lies between this wood and Moor Copse itself, creating a natural and interesting contrast. Moor Copse is an old coppiced ash wood with widely spaced oak and ash tree standards, where typical woodland plants such as early-purple orchid (4–6) are present.

Large numbers of moths (over 250 species) have been recorded. The handsome white admiral butterfly, which lays its eggs on the abundant honeysuckle, is seen on the wing in July and early August. Beetles and other invertebrates flourish in these woodlands, reflecting the large quantity of fallen and cut wood left to rot specifically for their benefit.

Muntjac, roe deer and foxes are regularly seen, while grass snakes bask in the sunshine of the newly cut woodland. A variety of woodland birds, including the sparrowhawk and tawny owl, can be seen here.

The River Pang itself must not be forgotten. Although the river has suffered greatly from low water flows and increasing pollution in recent summers, it is now improving.

Management
The rides are kept open and much of the woodland is in the process of being coppiced in rotation.

Moor Copse

OS sheet 175; SU 633738

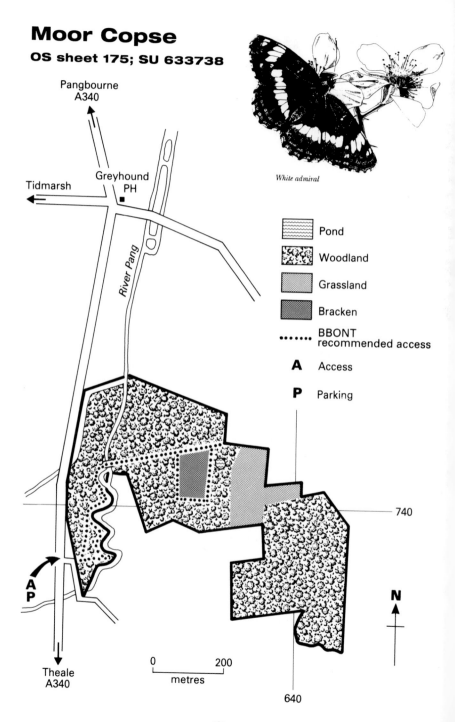

White admiral

Pangbourne
A340

Tidmarsh

Greyhound
PH

River Pang

Pond

Woodland

Grassland

Bracken

•••••• BBONT
recommended access

A   Access

P   Parking

740

640

A
P

N

0   200
metres

Theale
A340

Owlsmoor Bog & Heath

OS sheet 175; SU 845632

Nearest towns Sandhurst, Bracknell and Camberley

A mixture of heathland, bog and woodland, 26 hectares (64 acres) in area. It is part of the Sandhurst to Owlsmoor Bogs and Heaths SSSI and is owned by BBONT, having been bought in two lots in 1985 and 1986.

Location
From the centre of Sandhurst take the A321 east (towards Camberley) to the roundabout and turn left onto the A3095. Cross two roundabouts and take the left turning before the next roundabout. Park next to the electricity sub-station at SU 850629. The reserve is left of here. (BROADMOOR BOTTOM reserve can also be visited from here; see page 30). Alternatively use the District Council car park just south of Crowthorne at SU 838631 and walk along the bridleway just to the north, which forms the southern boundary for most of the reserve. Edgbarrow Woods alongside (also within the SSSI) is managed by Bracknell Forest Borough Council.

Access
Open to the public. Dogs must be kept under control and horses are allowed along the bridleway only.

Description
Together with the Broadmoor to Bagshot Woods and Heath SSSI (of which BROADMOOR BOTTOM reserve is a part), the Sandhurst to Owlsmoor Bogs and Heaths SSSI forms 60% of all the open heath and bog remaining in Berkshire.

The reserve lies mostly on acidic and infertile sandy soils. In the low lying areas, a thin layer of peat has formed, allowing bog to develop. An important plant in the development of a bog is bog moss or sphagnum. These bog mosses can more or less survive on the nutrients brought by rain. Their floppy stems create a living sponge which traps not only water but organic matter. The presence of the organic matter allows other bog plants to grow. One bog plant, the round-leaved sundew (6–8) has an additional method of gaining nutrients. It is carnivorous, feeding on small insects which it traps in its sticky hairs.

The reserve has bilberry (4–6) and three species of heather growing on drier ground. The emperor moth, a handsome relative of the silk moth, can be seen quickly skimming over the heather tussocks in the sunshine in May. Lizards, slow-worms and adders are most likely to be seen sunning themselves on the heath after emerging from hibernation in spring. Shy rather than dangerous, adders are likely to be well hidden by the time you reach the spot.

Birds recorded nesting on the heath include tree pipit, nightjar and stonechat. Many others nest in the woodland. The pine and birch woodland has interesting fungi in autumn.

Management
The heathland is gradually being cleared of scrub and trees. Light grazing by cattle has been introduced to help control the scrub.

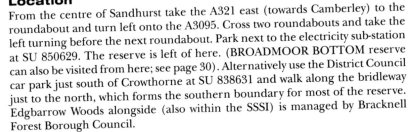

Owlsmoor Bog & Heath

OS sheet 175; SU 845632

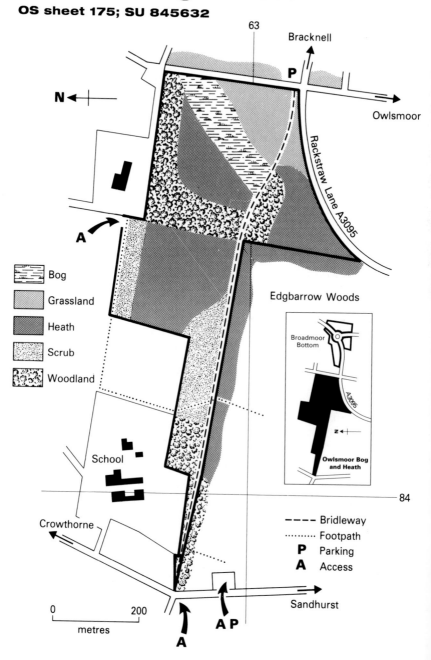

Bracknell

P

Owlsmoor

N ←

Rackstraw Lane A3095

A

Bog

Grassland

Heath

Scrub

Woodland

Edgbarrow Woods

Broadmoor
Bottom

A3095

Z ←

Owlsmoor Bog
and Heath

84

School

Crowthorne

---- Bridleway

.... Footpath

P Parking

A Access

0   200

metres

Sandhurst

A P

A

Rushbeds Wood & Lapland Farm

OS sheets 164 & 165; SP 672154

Nearest towns Aylesbury and Bicester

Of SSSI status, a woodland of 45 hectares (111 acres) bought in 1983, plus about 2.5 hectares (6 acres) of meadow. In 1985, BBONT also purchased Lapland Farm, 11 hectares (27 acres).

Location
From Aylesbury take the A41 towards Bicester. At Kingswood turn left along the unclassified road south-westwards to the T-junction. For Lapland Farm drive straight over and up the track in front, cross the railway bridge and park on hardstanding without obstructing the gates. To visit Rushbeds Wood turn left at the T-junction and just short of the next T-junction turn right up a track, through a gateway, across the railway bridge and park on the left. Please close the gate.

Access
The wood is open to the public along the rides. A public footpath crosses Lapland Farm. Please keep to it during the growing season and always keep dogs on a lead.

Description
Rushbeds Wood is an ancient woodland which appears on a map of 1590. It is one of the remaining woods of the ancient Forest of Bernwood, and has probably existed since just after the last Ice Age. Over 200 species of flowering plant, 50 fungi, and 60 bryophytes (mosses and liverworts) have been recorded. Woodland butterflies include white admiral, purple emperor and a colony of black hairstreak.

The large amount of dead wood provides good habitat for beetles and other invertebrates, which in turn attract numerous woodpeckers. Muntjac deer are common in the wood and foxes are seen frequently.

The two meadows of Lapland Farm have many species characteristic of ancient grassland, including greater burnet (flowers 6–9), dropwort (6–9) and pepper-saxifrage (6–9). Sprawling hedges are good for birds and butterflies. Two long, narrow meadows to the south of Rushbeds Wood are sheltered feeding sites for butterflies in summer and several ancient meadow plants, such as sneezewort (7–9), are found nowhere else on the reserve. All the meadows have abundant marbled white, meadow brown and common blue butterflies. Newts are found in both ponds. The hedge along the road, has many species of tree and shrub. Using the standard hedge-dating method (average number of species in 30 yards = age of the hedge in centuries), it is estimated to be at least 600 years old.

Management
Most of the trees were felled in the late 1940s and coppicing ceased soon after. Part of the wood is being coppiced again and much of the remainder will be left to grow gradually into a 'wildwood'. Glades have been created and rides widened to let in light and encourage more wild flowers and insects. The meadows at Lapland Farm are cut for hay in July and the regrowth is grazed, usually by sheep. The two narrow meadows are cut in July and grazed by cattle. The ancient hedge has been recently re-laid, mainly in two hedging competitions.

Rushbeds Wood & Lapland Farm

OS sheets 164 & 165; SP 672154

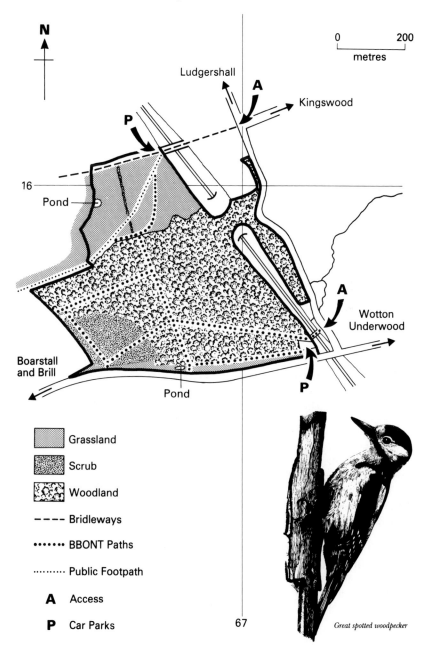

N

0   200
metres

Ludgershall

A

Kingswood

P

16

Pond

A

Wotton
Underwood

Boarstall
and Brill

Pond

P

Grassland

Scrub

Woodland

– – – – Bridleways

•••••• BBONT Paths

·········· Public Footpath

A Access

P Car Parks

67

Great spotted woodpecker

Stony Stratford

OS sheet 152; SP 785412

Nearest town Milton Keynes

A reinstated gravel working, 23 hectares (57 acres) in area. On lease from Milton Keynes Parks Trust and Milton Keynes Borough Council since 1982.

Location

From central Milton Keynes take the new A5 north to the roundabout and turn south towards Stony Stratford but then left along the bypass loop road and left at SP 790408 which ends at the car park.

Access

The northern part of the reserve and the path to the bird hide are open to the public. The reserve is a sanctuary for wildfowl and public access to the fenced area is restricted. A permit for the fenced area may be obtained from the BBONT office in Oxford.

Description

Parts of the reserve look like an ancient mere, plentifully fringed with reeds and with a richly varied population of wild geese, ducks and waders – the kind of place where Sir Peter Scott might have enjoyed painting. A photograph taken a few years ago shows that the site used to be an open meadow where redshank nested. However, under the grass lay deposits of good quality gravel, ideal for the new bypass about to be built nearby. The planners of Milton Keynes Development Corporation made the leap of imagination necessary to envisage a prize nature reserve within the boundaries of their new city. They realised that the gravel extraction could be an opportunity for, rather than a threat to, wildlife. If excavated to a prearranged design, the eventual flooding would produce a purpose-built wetland, with lagoons of varying depth and islands where wildfowl could nest safe from rats and foxes (and vandals of the human kind).

A deal was struck – the road builders were to have this local gravel and save on transport costs, while establishing an endowment fund to yield an income to help maintain the new reserve. The land was then leased to BBONT. Even before the last of the machinery left the site, waders, duck, geese, swans, grebes, moorhens and coots had moved in and started nesting.

BBONT's reserve warden and volunteers were involved from the start. An early diary entry shows that on one single day no fewer than 700 bur-reeds, 1,000 flowering rushes, 25 bulrushes and 100 yellow iris were planted by hand. The resulting look of instant maturity not only satisfied the birdlife, but also local residents who were then more willing to lend their moral support. Vandalism is still a problem, however – the hide has twice been burnt down, but restored afterwards. An artificial bank now houses a thriving colony of sand martins.

Management

Gravel must be brought in to maintain the islands. The public open space is mown, and grazed afterwards. Other areas are also grazed. There are many osier beds to coppice.

Stony Stratford

OS sheet 152; SP 785412

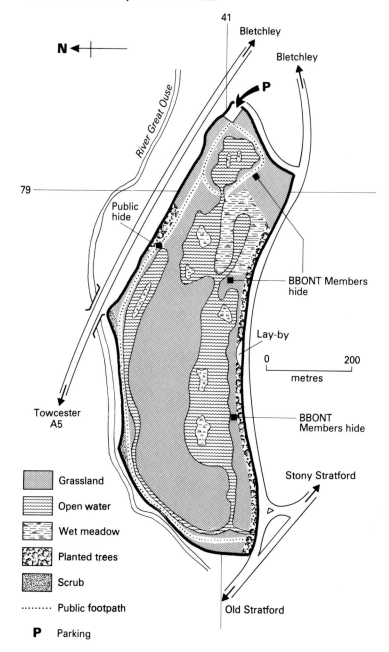

N ◄―┤―

41

Bletchley

Bletchley

River Great Ouse

P

79

Public hide

BBONT Members hide

Lay-by

0   200

metres

Towcester
A5

BBONT
Members hide

Stony Stratford

Grassland

Open water

Wet meadow

Planted trees

Scrub

.... Public footpath

P   Parking

Old Stratford

Sydlings Copse & College Pond

OS sheet 164; SP 559096

Nearest town Oxford

A varied, multi-habitat reserve of 16.8 hectares (42 acres), made up of two adjacent pieces of land. Sydlings Copse was bought from Brasenose College in 1977. College Pond is an adjoining area managed under an agreement with Christ Church, dated 1975. The whole site is part of a larger SSSI.

Location

From the Headington roundabout on the ring road, proceed northwards past the crematorium and turn left on the B4027. Go about 320 metres to a point opposite Royal Oak farmhouse. Park on the road verge and walk southwards along a bridleway for about 600 metres, past two pieces of woodland. Just past the second wood you will see another wood one field distant on your right. This is Sydlings Copse.

Access

The reserve is open to the public. Sydlings Copse has a wildlife walk to guide the visitor around its many habitats. Although both parts of the reserve are adjoining, there is no clear path from one to the other. The wildlife walk goes past the eastern end of College Pond, but the public footpath at the western end does not link up with Sydlings Copse.

Description

Despite its relatively small size, this reserve is one of the best botanical sites in midland Britain, largely because of the variety of habitats it contains. The habitats are crammed in a steeply-sided valley and include reedbed, fen, carr, a stream, broadleaved woodland, coniferous woodland and heath. There are also more open areas of grassland which (because of the underlying geology) provide interesting comparisons. Some areas have an acidic soil and here bracken and gorse can be seen, while the other grassy areas close by are over limestone and thus alkaline. In total over 400 plant species have been recorded on the reserve. One unusual plant seen in the north-eastern corner of the reserve is the toothwort (4–5), which is a strange, pale pink plant, parasitic on the roots of hazel.

The grassland is at its best in summer, with the greatest displays of wild flowers being seen in July. There is a myriad of wild flowers (over 120 have been recorded on this grassland alone). These include the large thyme (flowering 5–8), hairy violet (4) and woolly thistle (7–9). As a result of the number of species of wild flower, insect life is particularly good. In total, 28 species of butterfly and 149 species of moth have been recorded. Butterflies such as the marbled white, meadow brown, orange-tip and dark green fritillary are just a few of those attracted here. In addition, many moths such as burnets (day-flying red and black moths), grass emerald and July highflyer are also present.

Less colourful, but of equal importance, is the range of beetles found on the reserve. One example is the bloody-nosed beetle, so called because it exudes a red liquid if disturbed.

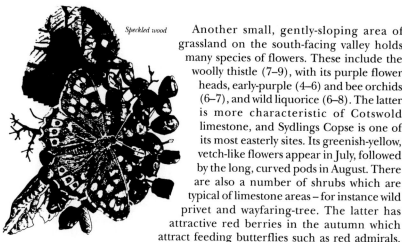
Speckled wood

Another small, gently-sloping area of grassland on the south-facing valley holds many species of flowers. These include the woolly thistle (7–9), with its purple flower heads, early-purple (4–6) and bee orchids (6–7), and wild liquorice (6–8). The latter is more characteristic of Cotswold limestone, and Sydlings Copse is one of its most easterly sites. Its greenish-yellow, vetch-like flowers appear in July, followed by the long, curved pods in August. There are also a number of shrubs which are typical of limestone areas – for instance wild privet and wayfaring-tree. The latter has attractive red berries in the autumn which attract feeding butterflies such as red admirals, commas and speckled woods.

The woodland itself is a contrast to the open grassland. It is host to a different variety of wildlife. The mixed, broadleaved woodland is dominated by oak and hazel, but also includes beech, hornbeam, sycamore and maple. These species suggest that the woodland has been here for some considerable time. This is reinforced by the presence of a number of smaller plants which are typical of ancient woodland, including herb-Paris (5–7) and wood spurge (4–5).

In spring, wood anemone (3–5), lesser celandine (3–5) and early dog-violet (3–5) can be found. Summer brings the large nettle-leaved bellflower (7–9). Dewberry, a close relative of the blackberry, is a pleasing sight in autumn.

In addition to the woodland plant species, there are also many different types of birds. All three types of woodpecker are present. Chiffchaffs and other warblers add their songs to the other sounds of the wood.

One of the reasons why Sydlings Copse and College Pond are so valuable is because of their examples of wetlands. Wetlands are one of the most threatened wildlife habitats in lowland Britain. They include ponds, marshes and, perhaps rarest of all, fens. Fens develop on waterlogged ground fed by alkaline water and where there is some accumulation of surface peat. The reserves' fenland is scattered along the stream. Its presence is probably due to activity by man. Studley Priory owned much of the area in the thirteenth century and it is likely that the stream was dammed in medieval times to create a fishpond. The pond has gradually silted up and the dam has long since been breached, creating a valley fen. There is also a large area of reedbed around College Pond, at the western end of the reserve.

Bog pimpernel

Although the fen is too wet and overgrown to enter, a view of it can be gained from the valley sides. In many ways it is fortunate that the fen is inaccessible, since such habitats are easily damaged by trampling. At least six species of dragonfly hunt across the fens, preying on the insects attracted to numerous wetland plants. The plants include the fen bedstraw (5–6), marsh pennywort (6–8), bog pimpernel (6–8), marsh helleborine (7–8) and columbine (5–7).

To the north of Sydlings Copse, a large block of conifer plantation has been clear felled as part of the ongoing heathland restoration project. This has exposed large patches of sandy, nutrient-poor soil, ideal for heathland species such as gorse and heather, while in areas of more stable soil, bracken and bramble have become first colonisers as the site gradually changes with time.

There is already a small patch of heathland at the top of the valley near the centre of the reserve. The geology of this area is complicated – limestone and sandy soils side by side. The heathland has developed on the sandy soil and has a number of species which are rare in Oxfordshire. These include the slender St John's-wort (7–9) and the pill sedge. The fly agaric is also present – a typical red and white toadstool.

Lizards can often be seen basking in the sunshine on stacked log piles on the chalk grassland. Grass snakes and slow-worms – the latter are actually legless lizards – can occasionally be glimpsed.

Many mammals such as grey squirrels, deer, bats and foxes also make their homes here. Grey squirrels were introduced into Britain last century and have ousted the native red squirrel. They often take bark from young trees, which can distort the growth of, or kill, the trees. Like deer, in large enough numbers they can be considered pests. The deer, although a beautiful addition to the copse, can stunt or kill young trees by nibbling the new shoots. Bats can be seen around the site at dusk and dawn. They hunt through woodland, over grassland and water, using echolocation to catch their quota of insects. The patient visitor may see foxes at the reserve. They often have regular runs. Foxes are omnivorous, their diets including berries as well as voles and beetles.

Management

The major management tool employed on the reserve is the sheep grazing which occurs both on the limestone grassland to the south of Sydlings Copse and on the heathland (including the restoration area) to the north. This aims to prevent scrub encroachment, a major threat to habitat continuity.

Encroachment is also a problem in the fen. Willow has to be removed on a regular basis to prevent both excessive shading and drying, whilst reed is cut in the summer to encourage the more unusual species in this unusual group of fen communities.

Sydlings Copse & College Pond
OS sheet 164; SP 559096

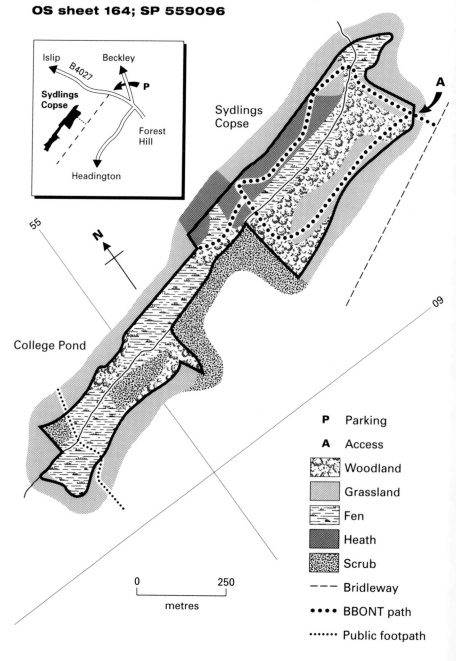

P — Parking
A — Access
Woodland
Grassland
Fen
Heath
Scrub
— — Bridleway
•••• BBONT path
••••••• Public footpath

0   250
metres

Tuckmill Meadow

OS sheet 174; SU 240900

Nearest towns Faringdon and Shrivenham

A meadow with a stream and a small spinney totalling 5.3 hectares (13½ acres). Due to its remnants of calcareous fen, it is an SSSI. It was bought by the Vale of the White Horse District Council (who fenced the boundaries) and is on lease to BBONT from them at £1 per annum. It was declared a Local Nature Reserve in 1992 (National Parks and Access to the Countryside Act 1949).

Location

From Faringdon take the A420 towards Swindon, turn off left for Watchfield. Follow this road towards Shrivenham past the Military College and as the road bends sharp left, turn right into the track past Shrivenham Park Golf Club. About 100 metres after passing the driveway to the Golf Club, there is a gate into a small car park, at SU 238897.

Access

Open to the public.

Description

The name 'Tuckmill' refers to a fulling mill which once stood on the northern bank of the brook. 'Tucking' is a local word for fulling – beating cloth in a mixture of fuller's earth and water to increase its density. (Fuller's earth is still dug locally at Baulking.) Power from the mill's water-wheel lifted the drop hammers for the processing.

The reserve's main attractions are an L-shaped meadow and most of the small spinney known as Ratcoombe Copse. The higher ground on the long arm of the meadow is limestone grassland with a large variety of wild flowers. Part of the relic fen lies along the stream in the long arm, marked by such typical plants as marsh-marigold (flowering 3–5) meadowsweet (6–9) and great willowherb (7–8). With stands of reed in places, the shorter arm is mainly marshy grassland and fen. One interesting feature of this part of the reserve is the old stream bed meandering across it. The wetter areas are good for dragonflies and damselflies (more needs to be known about the populations here) and kingfishers and herons have been seen. The brook forms part of the reserve.

Ratcoombe Copse lies on a slope above the fen and has a variety of shrubs, including guelder-rose (6–7). A bird hide at the lower end overlooks the fen.

The hedgerows around the meadow are rich in wildlife, providing a good habitat for invertebrates and hence a larder for breeding birds such as chiffchaffs and spotted flycatchers. Moorhens, sedge and reed warblers and reed buntings are known to nest on the reserve.

Management

The grasslands have suffered in the past through lack of management. The site is now grazed by cattle and it is hoped that plant, butterfly and other insect numbers will recover. Educational use of the reserve is increasing. Access is being improved.

Tuckmill Meadow

OS sheet 174; SU 240900

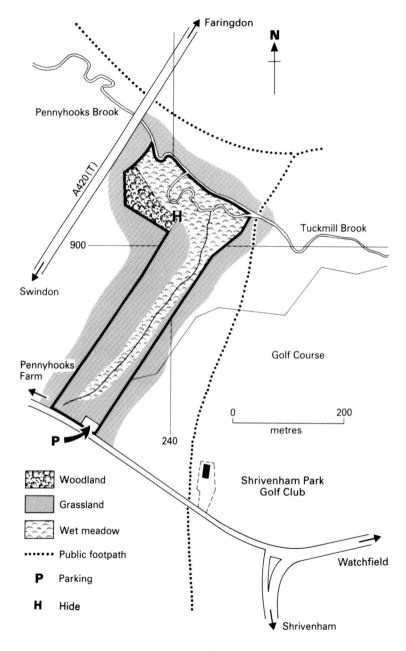

Faringdon

N

Pennyhooks Brook

A420(T)

900

Swindon

H

Tuckmill Brook

Pennyhooks
Farm

Golf Course

P

240

0   200

metres

Woodland

Grassland

Wet meadow

Public footpath

P   Parking

H   Hide

Shrivenham Park
Golf Club

Watchfield

Shrivenham

The Warburg Reserve

OS sheet 175; SU 720879

Nearest town Henley-on-Thames

A complex of woodland and grassland, 107 hectares (270 acres) in area. This reserve is the largest of BBONT's reserves. It is an SSSI and is in the Chilterns Area of Outstanding Natural Beauty. In 1967, 100 hectares (247 acres) of the reserve were bought by BBONT. The remainder were bought later.

Location

Leave Henley-on-Thames north-westwards on the A4130 and fork right at the end of the Fair Mile onto the B480. Turn second left just north of Middle Assendon and follow the twisty lane for two miles through a quiet valley. Shortly after the lane becomes a track, you reach the reserve. The car park is on the right. Please close the gate after you have entered the car park.

Alternative parking is at Maidengrove Common. There are entrances to the reserve nearby.

Access

Open to the public.

Description

The Warburg reserve is one of BBONT's most impressive sites. It lies on both slopes of a dry, winding valley cutting through the chalk and encompasses a complex mixture of woodland and grassland habitats with a wide variety of soil types and its own local climate. Although sheltered from gales, there may be unexpected frosts because of the pooling of cold air in the valley bottom. (Recordings of ground frost have occurred every month of the year at the reserve's climatological station). The steep slopes, thin soils and the frost pocket effect have meant that over the years, agriculture and forestry on the site have not been particularly successful, and the site has therefore not been subject to intensive farming use.

The main habitats are mixed broadleaved woodland, the trees being oak, ash, beech, birch, field maple and yew together with conifers from previous plantings. In addition there is beech woodland, conifer plantations of larch, spruce and Corsican pine, scrub and open grassland. Some of the woodland appears on maps of 1768, and these areas are likely to be ancient woodland, never having been cleared for fields.

The broadleaved woodlands have a rich variety of shrubs making up the understorey below the trees, while there are plentiful woodland wild flowers. In spring much of the woodland has spectacular numbers of wood anemones (3–5) and bluebells (4–6). Orchid species growing in the shaded conditions include narrow-lipped helleborine (7–8), broad-leaved helleborine (7–9), violet helleborine (8–9) and bird's-nest orchid (5–7). The woodland edge provides a different habitat. Typical plants found include yellow archangel (5–6), fly orchid (5–6), and common twayblade (5–7). In lightly wooded areas and along most woodland edges, common dog-violet (4–6) and early dog-violet (3–5) grow in abundance.

There are three types of grassland on the reserve – old grassland in existence since 1870, grassland which was planted with trees in the late 1800s and grassland created since 1967 when the reserve was bought. A flock of sheep is kept on the reserve to graze the grassland, maintaining the number of wild flowers. On the grassy rides and open grassland areas grow many wild flowers typical of chalk soils. These include pyramidal orchid (flowering 6–8), Chiltern gentian (7–9) and bird's-foot-trefoil (5–9), to name but a few. Some grassland plants, such as squinancywort (6–9), only occur where the soil overlaying the chalk is very thin. This occurs where rabbits have scraped or dug, and where the reserve's sheep have grazed extra closely. There is a small amount of acidic grassland or heathland on the reserve. On this area, gorse and heather have recently appeared.

In total, over 450 different species of higher plants have been recorded in the reserve, including 15 wild orchids and 50 plants which, in southern England, are usually found only in ancient woodland. No less than 850 species of fungi have been listed.

The reserve is not only diverse in terms of plants, but also animals. Records include 37 species of butterfly and 250 species of moth. Butterflies benefit from a number of different environments – woodlands, grasslands, rides – and there are many different species to look out for. In June and July, purple emperor, white admiral, silver-washed fritillary and dark green fritillary butterflies, among others, can be seen on the reserve. Among the many species of moth here are the maple prominent and the alder moth.

At least 34 different species of bird have nested here (and 75 species have been sighted in the reserve). There is usually a pair of sparrowhawks present. All three species of woodpecker are found and there are a good number of treecreepers and nuthatches. Less common are whitethroats and lesser whitethroats. The older conifers support goldcrests and crossbills. Woodcock fly above the reserve paths. They are related to waders and follow the rides much as their relatives might follow a river. At night tawny and long-eared owls can be seen.

Lizards, grass snakes and adders are all present at the reserve. Common lizards and slow-worms are reasonably common in all the grassy parts of the reserve. The grass snake occurs in much smaller numbers but occupies the same sites. Adders are the most restricted, mainly confined to two areas of the reserve.

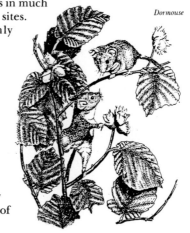

Dormouse

Amphibians such as the smooth newt and common frog have bred regularly in the artificial ponds.

Dormice live and hibernate on the reserve. Areas of trees are coppiced – the trees are cut down to almost ground level, the stumps then regenerate and the trees grow back more bushy than before. Dormice spend much of the time in the bushy coppiced trees, rarely touching the ground. Hazel coppice is particularly popular. In the autumn, with the prospect of hibernating, the dormice fatten up on hazelnuts. In winter they hibernate in nests, usually about a metre from the ground.

Hares are regular sights in fields around the reserve and are quite often seen in parts of the reserve's woodlands which adjoin fields. They have bred at least once in the reserve. Rabbits, voles, shrews and moles are also present.

Muntjac, roe and fallow deer live on and around the reserve. Fallow and roe deer are native species, while the muntjac deer has been introduced. Muntjac deer have a characteristic bark sounding almost like that of a dog's, except there is one bark every 5–8 seconds.

Although beautiful, deer can become pests in large numbers. Browsing by deer has prevented some of the ash coppice regenerating. The muntjac deer appear to be the main culprits, hiding in small patches of bramble near to newly coppiced areas and chewing the new shoots.

Other mammals seen at the reserve include pipistrelle bats which can be seen flying through the trees at dusk and dawn. These mammals use echolocation to catch midges and small moths. They send out a high pitched squeak, too high for humans to hear, and listen for the echo. The echo tells them the exact location of their prey.

The reserve caters for visitors as well as plants and animals. There is an interpretative centre and a nature trail for visitors. Trail guides and lists of plants and animals are available. The nature trail takes visitors on a walk through many of the different habitats. The site is regularly visited by botanists, birdwatchers, scientists, students and schoolchildren. A small area of the site is now accessible to people in wheelchairs. The wheelchair access is from the car park to the pond and bird hide by the interpretative centre. A ramp to the centre is also in place. Disabled visitors and groups wishing to visit the reserve should book in advance with the Warden, Warden's House, Bix Bottom, Henley-on-Thames, Oxfordshire. Telephone 01491 641727.

Management

The aim is to maintain the variety of habitats while expanding the area of chalk grassland. Management includes coppicing the woodland and the removal of alien trees such as sycamore, Turkey oak and some of the conifers. Fences of 'brashings' – small branches and twigs – have been placed around newly coppiced trees to prevent the deer eating the new shoots. The new growth from coppiced trees, hazel in particular, is quite straight and flexible. This means that it can be used to make woven barriers known as wattle hurdles which can be used around the reserve.

Forty hectares of the reserve have been chosen for non-intervention. The trees will be left uncut and undisturbed. This area will eventually resemble ancient woodland, with trees of varying ages. Short rotation scrub management is carried out at the reserve to benefit the lizards and snakes.

The sheep flock is moved around the reserve in a planned rotation, grazing the grasslands as necessary to keep down the coarse grasses. The flock is removed at certain times to allow the wild flowers to flower and seed themselves.

Recently, 3 hectares of improved (fertilized) pasture have been acquired. These will be grazed by the sheep flock and will not have insecticides or fertilizers added. The land should gradually become less fertile and revert to flower-rich meadowland.

The Warburg Reserve

OS sheet 175; SU 720879

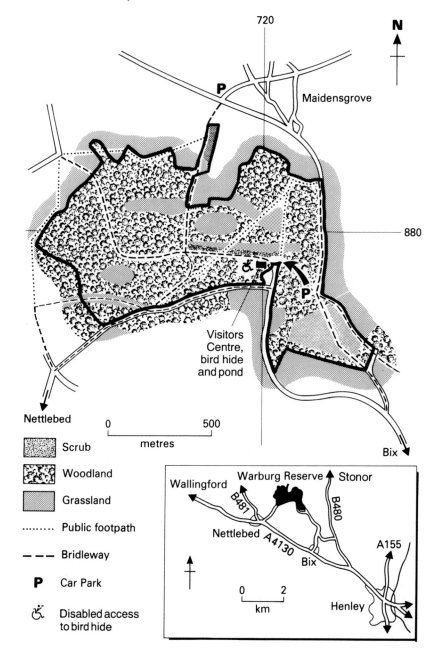

N

720

Maidensgrove

880

Visitors Centre, bird hide and pond

P

Nettlebed

0   500
metres

Bix

Scrub

Woodland

Grassland

.... Public footpath

– – – Bridleway

P   Car Park

&   Disabled access to bird hide

Wallingford

Warburg Reserve   Stonor

B481

B480

Nettlebed   A4130

Bix

A155

Henley

0   2
km

Wells Farm
OS sheet 164; SP 620008

Nearest town Oxford

A 66 hectare (163 acre) mixed farm leased to BBONT for 999 years in 1990.

Location
Take the B480 east from Oxford to Stadhampton. Turn left onto the A329 to Little Milton. Go past the Plough Inn, up the hill and turn sharp right. The farmyard entrance is the left, next to the telephone box.

Access
Open to the public. Dogs must be kept on leads at all times.

Description
Wells Farm gets its name from the great number of springs that emerge on the valley side. It has been mainly open farmland since the fifteenth century. Although it was intensively farmed in the recent past, it still has considerable wildlife value. As a mixed working farm, it demonstrates a combination of modern farming practices and practical conservation.

Most of the farmland is open fields, divided between sheep-grazed pasture and arable land. The fields are edged by 3 metre wide field margins which have been sown with a wild flower seed mixture. New flowers such as field pansy (5–6), scarlet pimpernel (5–10) and field forget-me-not (4–10) give a contrast of colour to the field crops and help to encourage orange-tip and peacock butterflies to take to the air during summer.

In addition, there is a 6 metre wide grassy bank crossing the arable fields from north to south. This has been sown with a variety of tufted grasses which provide cover for spiders and beetles. These are encouraged as they prey on aphids and therefore help to protect the crops naturally.

From the three circular walks, each of a different length, extensive views of the Chilterns can be enjoyed, as well as views of the village and church of Little Milton to the west, and the Old Mill of Great Haseley to the east.

In the valley bottom a small tree-lined brook links two ponds at either end of the farm. The brook contains watercress (5–10), great willowherb (6–8), yellow iris (6–8) and lesser spearwort (6–10). It is lined by willow pollards and scrub.

The ponds are in the process of silting up, while both are surrounded by spinneys of old ash and hazel coppice, with a mixture of oak, wild cherry, alder and other deciduous trees. With a reedbed and willow carr around the eastern pond, a rich and varied cover has been created. This plays host to a large amount of wildlife, ranging from frogs and toads, foxes and squirrels, through chaffinches, linnets, coots and moorhens, to holly blue butterflies. Reeds, water mint (7–9), and marsh-marigolds (3–5) attract numerous insects to the pond areas, providing food for brown hawker and broad-bodied chaser dragonflies among others.

Management
BBONT's main aim is to run the farm both profitably and in harmony with wildlife. There is an emphasis on habitat creation. Rotational pollarding of willows is undertaken, as is much habitat maintenance work.

Wells Farm

OS sheet 164; SP 620008

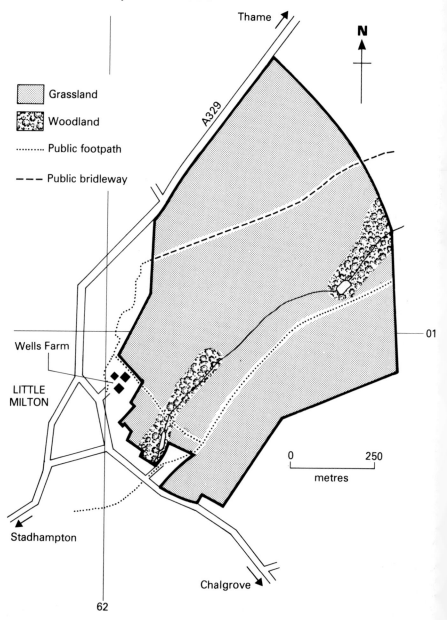

Open access nature reserves

Abbey Fishponds
Asham Meads
Aston Clinton Ragpits
Avery's Pightle
Blackwater Reach Meadow
Blenheim Farm
Bray Pit
Buckingham Canal
Burrows Reserve, Bernwood
Buttler's Hangings
Cholsey Marsh
Cowcroft
Glyme Valley
Gomm Valley
Harry Williams'/Lamb's Pool Reserve
Hartslock
Haymill Valley
Homefield Wood
Hook Norton Railway Cutting
Horley
Hornton Meadows
Hungerford Marsh
Hurley Chalk Pit
Iffley Meadows
Inkpen Crocus Field
Long Grove Wood
Long Herdon & Grange Meadows
Millfield Wood
Northerams Wood
Oakley Hill
Oxey Mead
Pilch Field
Pitstone Hill
Seven Barrows
The Slade, Bloxham
Sole Common Pond
Vicarage Pit
Warren Bank
Watts Reserve (White Shute)
Weston Turville Reservoir
Westwell Gorse
Whitecross Green Wood
Wildridings Copse
Woodsides Meadow, Wendlebury

Abbey Fishponds

OS sheet 164; SU 512981

Nearest town Abingdon

A 7 hectare (17 acre) relic wetland habitat, notable for areas of reedbed and wet meadow. It is subleased by BBONT from the Vale of the White Horse District Council.

Location

As the map shows, the reserve lies to the south of the Abingdon to Radley road. It is about ¾ mile from the junction of the Radley road with the A4183 Oxford road. There is parking in the streets nearby. The access points are shown on the map.

Access

Open to the public. Footpaths cross the reserve (see the map opposite).

Description

In medieval times fishponds were an important food resource for any country community. Religious rules forbade red meat on Friday, but people were allowed to eat fish instead. A village would usually have its specially dug fishponds, and a monastic community a more elaborate set. The fish they supplied (usually carp) were a valuable source of protein.

Most of those ponds have now disappeared. We see here the remains of the medieval embankments raised to dam the stream. There is little open water today, however, but some areas of reedbed, fen and wet meadow remain. Reed buntings are sometimes seen, and their chirruping song heard. Although preferring dense reedbeds for nesting, these birds are also attracted to the cover given by scrub. In fact the bulk of the area has dried out, and the drier ground carries taller growth, scrub and even woodland.

There are wide stands of great willowherb with its reddish purple flowers (flowering 7–8). Greater botanical interest, however, lies with the more colourful flowers such as the bright yellow marsh-marigold (3–5) and yellow iris (5–7). However, the purplish southern marsh-orchid (6–8), once plentiful on the reserve, may now be extinct here.

The reserve boasts many damselflies. Those recorded at various periods in the summer are banded, azure, common blue, blue-tailed and emerald damselflies. The common darter dragonfly is also seen. Dragonflies are more robust than damselflies. They rest with wings held open while damselflies fold theirs back. Darter dragonflies hunt their prey of winged flies (or even damselflies) by darting from a perch. The larger hawker dragonflies hunt while flying on patrol.

Management

The open grassland needs to be regularly cut to keep down the coarse grasses which would otherwise swamp the wild flowers. The reedbed is cut rotationally to encourage it to grow vigorously and the bramble thickets likewise to encourage blackberry production.

Abbey Fishponds

OS sheet 164; SU 512981

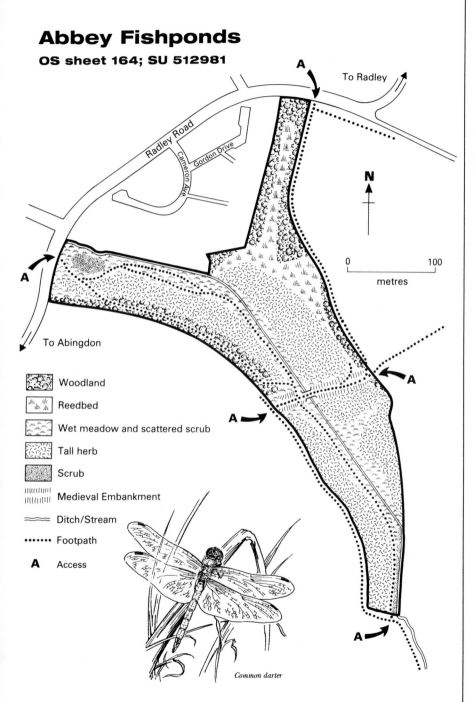

To Radley

To Abingdon

N

0   100
metres

Woodland

Reedbed

Wet meadow and scattered scrub

Tall herb

Scrub

Medieval Embankment

Ditch/Stream

Footpath

A   Access

Radley Road

Cameron Ave

Gordon Drive

Common darter

Asham Meads

OS sheet 164; SP 590146

Nearest towns Oxford and Bicester

Three old meadows and a more recent oak plantation, totalling 22.8 hectares (56 acres) in area. This SSSI was bought by BBONT in 1987.

Location

From the A40 (Headington) roundabout on the eastern Oxford by-pass take the minor road north-east to Horton-cum-Studley. Leave the village as for Murcott and Bicester, turning left alongside the motorway. Half a mile past the right turn to Arncott, turn left down the track past Manor and Whitecross Green Farms. Please park in the reserve car park and not on the track.

Access

Open to the public at all times. Please keep dogs on leads when the meadows are being grazed during autumn and early winter.

Description

The reserve consists of three meadows, Upper Marsh, Lower Marsh and Rowbotham. These appear to have the same boundaries as shown on a map of 1590. They are thought to have belonged to the lost Otmoor village of Nash, from which the name of Asham has been derived.

Unlike modern meadows, which have heavy applications of fertilizers and pesticides, these are 'unimproved' and have a rich variety of grasses and flowering plants. The varying history and soil conditions of each field result in differing plant communities. Upper and Lower Marsh are dominated by crested dog's-tail grass (in flower 6–7) and black (common) knapweed (6–9). Rowbotham, however, has meadow foxtail grass (5–6) and the attractive great burnet (6–9). Other plants also show local preferences, with green-winged orchids (4–6) and dyer's greenweed found in Upper Marsh while the wetter Rowbotham has good colonies of devil's-bit scabious (6–10), ragged-Robin (5–7) and lesser spearwort (5–9).

The 'ridge and furrow' produced by ploughing is possibly the effect of fairly recent attempts at drainage, but modern drainage of the neighbouring fields has had a far more drastic effect on the water table. Even the boundary ponds are empty for much of the year, though the central one does remain full and supports several species of dragonfly including the four-spotted chaser and the emperor.

Behind the central pond are the remains of an old withy bed that almost certainly supplied willow osiers for the eel fisheries on the River Ray. The small oak wood was probably planted in the thirties, and the surrounding scrub (and the reserve's hedges) support good populations of invertebrates and breeding birds. The nightingale is an occasional visitor and the rare black hairstreak butterfly has been recorded on this site.

Management

BBONT is continuing the traditional management of late hay cutting followed by autumn grazing by sheep.

Asham Meads

OS sheet 164; SP 590146

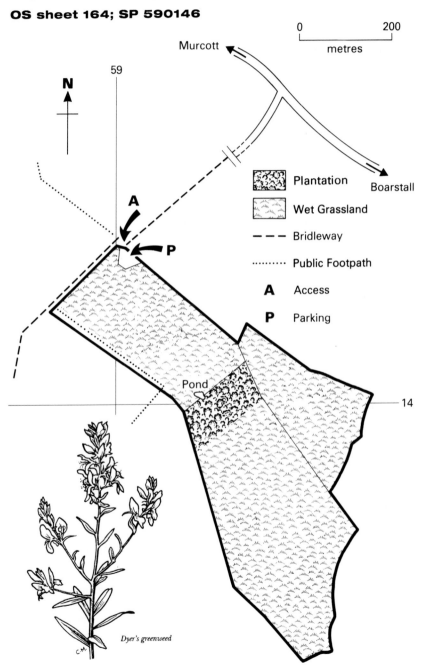

Murcott

0   200
metres

59

N

Boarstall

	Plantation
	Wet Grassland
– – –	Bridleway
....	Public Footpath
A	Access
P	Parking

A

P

Pond

14

Dyer's greenweed

Aston Clinton Ragpits

OS sheet 165; SP 887107

Nearest towns Tring and Wendover

A small area of old chalk pits 2.4 hectares (6 acres) in total. It is an SSSI. BBONT owns 2.1 acres and manages the remainder under an agreement with Aston Clinton Parish Council.

Location

From Wendover take the A4011 towards Tring. After 2¼ miles, turn right onto an unclassified road towards St Leonards. After 60 metres, park on the left hand verge. Entry to the reserve is over the railings next to the double iron gates.

Access

Open to the public, but no dogs please.

Description

This is a small but varied area of old pits at the foot of the Chiltern escarpment, which was once worked for superior quality chalk freestone or 'rag' used for local building. When work ceased, plants and animals from the countryside around colonised the site and as a result it now boasts a rich variety of wild flowers, shrubs and animal life. Paradoxically, many of these invading species have now been driven from the surrounding countryside by unsympathetic land management.

The woodland fringe to the west, predominantly beech and yew, serves as a useful screen. The rest of the reserve is grassland and scrub, mainly hawthorn (flowering 5–6) and dogwood (5–7) but also buckthorn (5–6), spindle (5–6), guelder-rose (6–7) and wayfaring-tree (5–6). These shrubs have attractive berries later in the year, providing food for birds.

Thirty-one species of butterfly have been recorded, many of them linked with the grassland which is a botanist's delight. The wild flower species include cowslips (flowering 4–5), bright blue chalk milkwort (5–6), purple autumn gentian (8–9), yellow horseshoe vetch (5–7), and nine species of orchids. The orchids are at their best in June and July.

There is a population of slow-worms. Slow-worms are neither slow, nor worms, but are in fact legless lizards which feed mainly on slugs. Superficially, they resemble snakes. When frightened, in common with other lizards, they shed their tails and run away, leaving their wriggling tails behind to distract predators. The harmless grass snake, a true snake, may also be seen on the reserve.

Management

The aim is to maintain the variety of habitats here. The grassland within the pits has been fenced and is periodically grazed by sheep. The sheep prevent coarse grasses from taking over and smothering the wild flowers. Scrub has been cleared (the dogwood is a problem as it produces suckers when cut). Mowing is carried out to stop scrub invading the open ground. Some lengths of hedgerow have been cut and 'laid', the trunks being partially cut through, bent over and interwoven with others.

Aston Clinton Ragpits

OS sheet 165; SP 887107

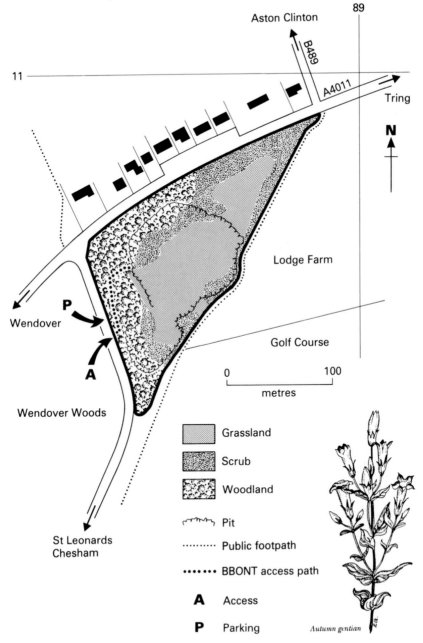

Aston Clinton

B489

A4011

Tring

11

N

Lodge Farm

P

Wendover

Golf Course

A

0   100

metres

Wendover Woods

St Leonards
Chesham

Grassland

Scrub

Woodland

Pit

Public footpath

BBONT access path

A   Access

P   Parking

Autumn gentian

Avery's Pightle

OS sheet 174; SU 435651

Nearest town Newbury

An old flower-rich meadow, 1.3 hectares (3.18 acres) in area. This SSSI was bought by BBONT in 1985.

Location

To find this reserve, you need to locate Enborne, just to the west of Newbury. At the east end of the village, Church Lane leaves southwards towards Crockham Heath. After ½ mile this road crosses a small stream, and the reserve is on the right-hand side past (to the south of) the stream. Please park off the narrow road.

Access

Open to the public. Dogs are not allowed on the reserve when cattle are grazing in late summer and early autumn.

Description

'Pightle' (pronounced to rhyme with title) is a medieval word for a small enclosed meadow. Such fields were once a part of every village, but in recent times most of them have been drained, deep-ploughed and fertilized for high yield grasses or grain.

Traces of an ancient ridge and furrow system show that this field has not been ploughed for hundreds of years. The fact that herbicides and artificial fertilizers have not been applied is shown by the sheer variety of plant life: 113 species of flowering plants plus 24 wild grasses, sedges and rushes have been recorded. It is a mistake to think that the application of fertilizers will result in more flowers. What happens is the reverse. The new supply of nutrient encourages the taller coarse plants to get ahead and swamp the other species!

Sixteen plants normally confined to ancient grasslands are seen here. They are unevenly distributed across the field, reflecting differences in drainage management. In spring, on the drier, shorter grazed area to the south, look for adder's-tongue, a small fern which, with its small spathe and 'tongue', looks like a green Lords-and-Ladies. Here pepper-saxifrage (flowering 6–8) and sneezewort (7–8) also grow, whereas dyer's greenweed (6–8), meadow thistle (6–8) and betony (6–9) are seen on the wetter ground to the north.

There are also wild orchids – the scrubby area near the stream in the north-east corner holds a colony of broad-leaved helleborine (7–9).

It is a particularly rich place for butterflies and birds. Butterflies seen here include large and small skipper, orange-tip, meadow brown, common blue and green-veined white. Other insects abound.

Birds which have been noted included lapwing and blackcap, lesser whitethroat, yellowhammer and a variety of warblers attracted by the hedgerows. Some of these regularly nest here.

Management

In the past, before becoming a BBONT reserve, it was grazed by ponies. It is now grazed by cattle.

Avery's Pightle

OS sheet 174; SU 435651

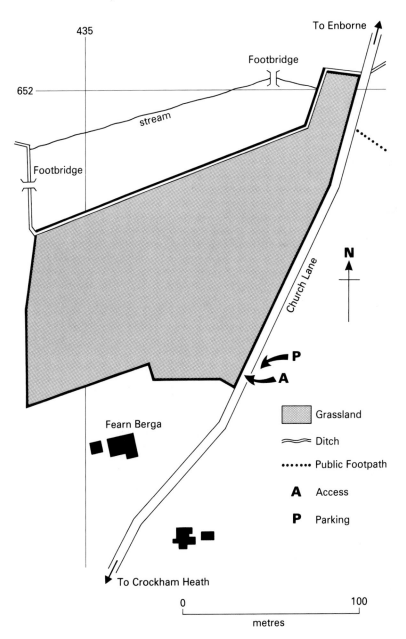

435

652

To Enborne

Footbridge

stream

Footbridge

Church Lane

N

P

A

Fearn Berga

To Crockham Heath

Grassland

Ditch

Public Footpath

A   Access

P   Parking

0   100

metres

Blackwater Reach Meadow

OS sheet 175; SU 843608

Nearest town Sandhurst

An 'unimproved' rough meadow of 1.2 hectares (3 acres). Part of the Blackwater Valley SSSI, it forms a section of the Sandhurst Memorial Park. It has been managed by BBONT in agreement with Sandhurst Town Council since 1985.

Location
It lies within Sandhurst. Leaving the town centre on the A321 towards Camberley, you will come to the Town Council offices and playing fields on your right. Park here and walk south to the River Blackwater. The reserve is the last field before the river, beyond a small lake.

Access
Open to the public. The footpath around the reserve is suitable for disabled access.

Description
A high quality, rough wet meadow, unimproved (that is, unchanged) by modern farming. Purple moor-grass and betony (flowering 6–9) are seen. These are two examples of a number of plants which are seldom found outside unimproved meadows and reflect a long period of uninterrupted grassland management without the use of fertilizers or pesticides.

Over 100 species of wild flowers have so far been recorded. The list includes ragged-Robin (flowering 5–6) and meadowsweet (6–9) growing in the marshier areas. The scent of the latter wafts across the reserve on still, humid summer evenings. Among the other flowers to interest the visitor are cuckooflower or lady's smock (4–5), yellow iris (5–7), tormentil (6–9), water forget-me-not (5–8) and four species of buttercup, mainly flowering in June.

With such a variety of plants comes a range of insect and other invertebrate life. The butterflies make the reserve a delight. One of the pleasures of the traditional countryside was to be able to walk through butterfly fields like this one, but such places are now hard to find.

Amongst the butterfly species here are orange-tip (which often lays its egg on cuckooflower), green-veined white (which may choose the same species of plant) and common blue. The latter is worth looking out for. It lays its eggs on various plants of the pea family and is widespread throughout Britain, but is not seen in large numbers in any one place.

The strongly flying large white and peacock butterflies have also been seen here, presumably breaking a journey to feed on the nectar of the flowers. Water measurers and great diving beetles have been recorded in the central ditch and grass snakes have been seen nearby.

The kingfisher is one of the birds recorded on the reserve.

Management
Areas are now cut in rotation in late summer.

Blackwater Reach Meadow

OS sheet 175; SU 843608

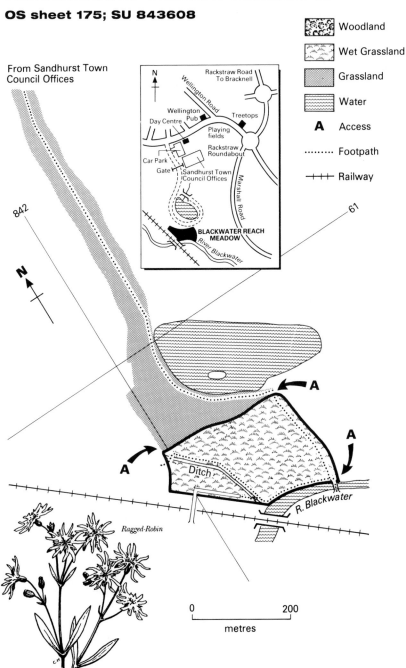

From Sandhurst Town
Council Offices

Woodland

Wet Grassland

Grassland

Water

A Access

.... Footpath

++++ Railway

N

842

61

N

A

A

A

Ditch

R. Blackwater

Ragged-Robin

0   200

metres

(inset map)

N

Rackstraw Road
To Bracknell

Wellington Road

Wellington
Pub

Treetops

Day Centre

Playing
fields

Rackstraw
Roundabout

Car Park

Gate

Sandhurst Town
Council Offices

Marshall Road

BLACKWATER REACH
MEADOW

River Blackwater

Blenheim Farm

OS sheet 164; SP 365195

Nearest town Charlbury

A field of 0.5 hectare (1¼ acres) which allows BBONT to demonstrate various management techniques. It was given to BBONT in 1987 by the Porter family.

Location

Approaching Charlbury from Oxford or Witney, by-pass the centre by following the main road around the east of the town. The road plunges down a steep hill, on the right of which are lay-bys for parking. Blenheim Farm House is in the bottom of the valley. A public footpath runs beside it, up the valley and through the reserve.

Access

Open to the public.

Description

The field lies at the top of a dry Jurassic limestone valley. It is bordered by hedgerows and a small, scrubby woodland which is good for warblers and other songbirds. Species heard include the blackcap with a rich melodious song, and the chiffchaff. The song of the latter, a repetitive 'tsip tsap tsap tsip', is hardly musical, but welcome for all that as this bird is a reliable herald of spring, usually first heard at the end of March.

The old hedges contain many species of trees and shrubs including field maple and crab apple. The true wild crab apple is often rather thorny, with blossom appearing in May. Its small round apples are yellowish, sometimes flushed with red, and very sour. Dogwood and spindle are also seen in these hedges, reflecting the limey nature of the soil here.

This sheltered valley has grasses and flowers typical of alkaline to neutral conditions, such as cowslips (flowering 4–5), lady's bedstraw (7–8) and common knapweed (6–8). Butterflies enjoy its warmth – blues are common and the orange-tip comes to the few cuckooflowers (4–5). Muntjac hide in the undergrowth.

The owners gave the field to BBONT as they wished to ensure the survival of the area as an 'unimproved' meadow available for people to use for walks, study and enjoyment. For some time BBONT had been discussing the possibility of setting up some 'Community Nature Reserves' in the three counties – reserves which need not be of great conservation value, but are near a town or village and accessible to local people. These reserves would be run by and for the local community.

Management

The grass is cut annually but some areas are mown more often. This provides different conditions for flowering plants. There are also bare ground plots, directly sown with seeds from local sources, another method of encouraging plant diversity.

Blenheim Farm

OS sheet 164; SP 365195

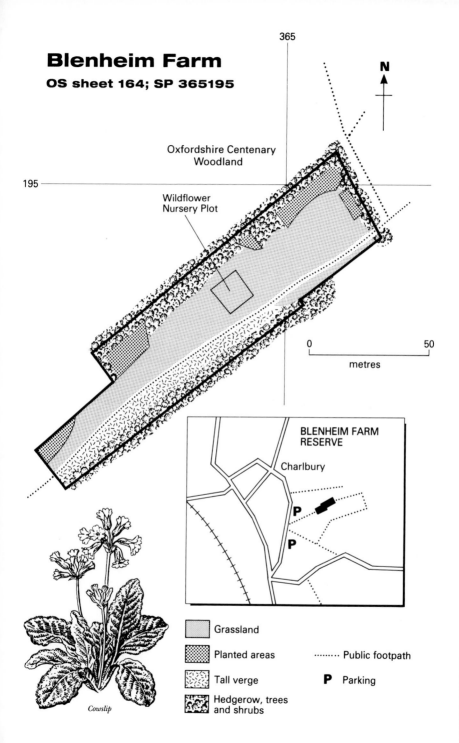

365

195

Oxfordshire Centenary
Woodland

Wildflower
Nursery Plot

N

0   50

metres

BLENHEIM FARM
RESERVE

Charlbury

P

P

Grassland

Planted areas

Tall verge

Hedgerow, trees
and shrubs

.... Public footpath

P Parking

Cowslip

Bray Pit
OS sheet 175; SU 906787

Nearest town Maidenhead

An old gravel working, now flooded, with varied surroundings. The reserve is 1.8 hectares (4.5 acres) in area and held on a peppercorn lease from the Summerlease Gravel Company Ltd.

Location

Leave Maidenhead southwards on the A308 through Bray Wick and under the M4. Turn left immediately after the Brayfield Arms hotel into Monkey Island Lane. Drive down this road past the Bray Marina on your right and after a further 100 metres turn left (through a gate) into the water sports area. Continue past the Sailboard Clubhouse and park at the end.

Access

Open to the public.

Description

This is a small, wet sand and gravel working with a strip of woodland on its east side and wide grassy banks on the north-west and south-west sides. Beyond a mature hedge the M4 motorway forms the north-west boundary.

This reserve is an example of what can be created with modest resources. It has a plant count of over 100 species; many wild flowers have been planted in the meadow areas around the pit, giving a splendid display throughout the summer. Species include oxeye daisy (flowering 5–9), chicory (6–9), common toadflax (6–10), greater knapweed (6–8), field scabious (6–10), restharrow (7–9), meadowsweet (6–9), betony (6–9), greater spearwort (8–9), meadow cranesbill (6–9) and sneezewort (7–8). The latter is a characteristic plant of old meadows.

Trees and shrubs have also been planted – wild cherry, wild pear and plum, alder and dogwood among them.

Over 20 species of butterfly have been recorded. On the wing in spring are green-veined white and orange-tip. In summer, common blue, three species of skipper and meadow brown can be seen. The meadow brown was once the emblem of long grass, but it is now much less common in today's intensively farmed countryside. Those familiar garden visitors, the peacock, red admiral and small tortoiseshell butterflies, are regularly seen here.

Bird life includes the grey heron, great crested grebe, moorhen, coot, and most notably the kingfisher. (Also of note are the common sandpiper, ringed plover and little ringed plover. The last is a summer visitor attracted to the shores of flooded gravel pits such as this).

A variety of dragonfly species can be seen. Bats hunt at dusk and dawn between the trees and over the open water. Nests of the harvest mouse have been found but these enchanting little rodents have yet be seen.

Management

Planting of various (and sometimes unusual) vegetation is undertaken, as mentioned above. Grass is cut and removed to simulate hay-making. This prevents the many wild flowers from being shaded out by the coarse, taller vegetation.

Bray Pit

OS sheet 175; SU 906787

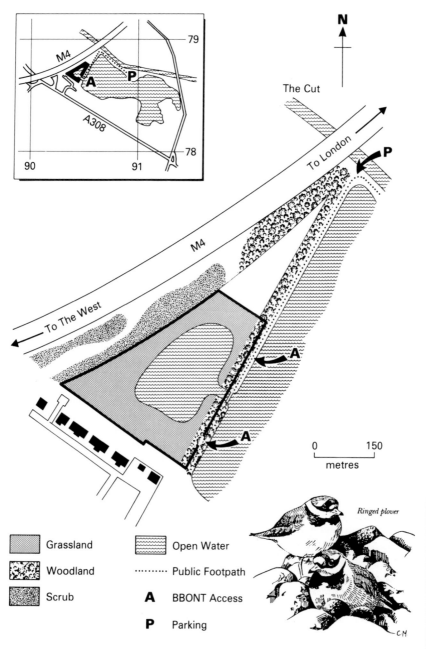

Grassland

Woodland

Scrub

Open Water

.... Public Footpath

A BBONT Access

P Parking

Ringed plover

Buckingham Canal

OS sheet 152; SP 726350

Nearest town Buckingham

A length of disused canal, 1 hectare (2.65 acres) in total. It was bought by BBONT in 1972.

Location

To reach the reserve, take the A422 east from Buckingham for 2 miles until you reach a farm track on the right, leading to a pumping house (Anglian Water). Members of the public should park near here and proceed on foot. BBONT members, however, may drive down the track, and just before the pumping house go through the gate on the left and park in the field adjoining Hyde Lane Gravel Pit. (Padlock key available from Seahawk Supplies, 4 Castle Street, Buckingham, £2 deposit. Please indicate that you are a BBONT member.) Then walk down past the pumping house and cross over to the canal towpath. The reserve begins after about 100 metres.

Access

Do not disturb the anglers at Hyde Lane Lake. Note that the sides of the canal lock are high and could be a hazard to unsupervised children.

Description

This reserve includes both banks of the disused canal, from the point of entry along to the disused lock and on past it to a bridge.

Sites abandoned by people can become of high wildlife interest and this disused canal is a case in point. The canal bed at the western end is dry but pools of water are found towards the eastern end. Just beyond the lock, the overflow from the gravel pit has created a piece of open water. Further along, the site has become overgrown with emergent aquatic plants until, just before the bridge, there is again open water.

These varied conditions, shallow pools and deeper water, provide a sanctuary for aquatic life, especially as shallow ponds are now hard to find in today's countryside. Most of the old field pools have been filled in (nowadays if cattle or sheep are grazing, water is piped in) and many wetlands have been drained. As a result, even the 'common' frog, which prefers shallow water, now has its breeding stronghold in the ponds of suburban gardens rather than in the countryside.

At this reserve, there is the haphazard, sheltered aquatic habitat of a kind once common everywhere. Frogs, toads, and colourful damselflies and dragonflies make use of it and the open water of the flooded gravel pit nearby. Grass snakes are also seen here – they swim well and hunt frogs and other aquatic life. Unusual birds recorded here have included the bittern and water rail.

Management

Future work needs to concentrate on such tasks as the removal of scrub along the canal banks and pollarding the willows near the lock in order the maintain the areas of open water. The hedge along the southern boundary needs to be trimmed down to let more light onto the water. The creation of more pools along the bed of the canal would be beneficial.

Buckingham Canal

OS sheet 152; SP 726350

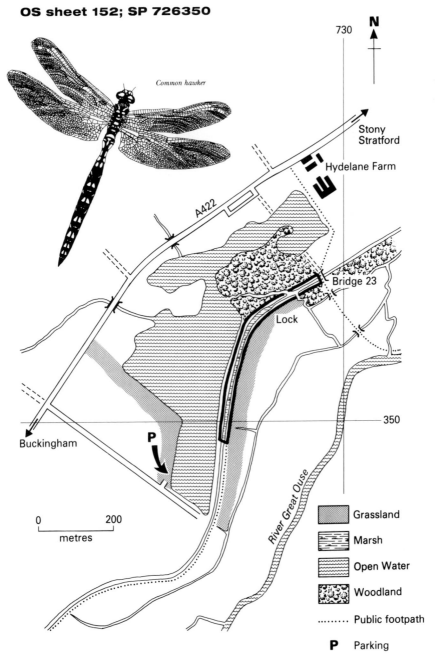

Common hawker

N

730

Stony Stratford

Hydelane Farm

A422

Bridge 23

Lock

Buckingham

350

River Great Ouse

P

0   200
metres

Grassland

Marsh

Open Water

Woodland

.... Public footpath

P   Parking

Burrows Reserve, Bernwood

OS sheet 164 & 165; SP 624114

Nearest town Oxford

A small block of scrub with some oak trees, 0.29 hectares (0.725 acres) in extent. BBONT bought the land in 1966. It was notified as part of the Shabbington Wood complex SSSI in 1987.

Location

From Headington roundabout on Oxford's eastern ring road, take the road north past the crematorium; turn right, cross to the B4027 and proceed to Stanton St John. Take the first left in the village. Fork left at the road junction at Menmarsh, and after ¾ mile there is a large car park on the right (SP 611117). From here walk along the Forestry Commission ride in Oakley Wood for a mile and turn left along another ride just after the deep water pond. The reserve lies at the end.

Access

Open to the public.

Description

The reserve was bought for its colony of black hairstreak butterflies. Conservation must often be directed to provide for special needs of wildlife which are endangered, and this butterfly provides a good example.

The female lays her eggs singly on blackthorn (sloe) and the caterpillars eat the leaves. In late spring (the year's weather influences the exact date) each caterpillar spins onto the side of a twig and changes into a chrysalis. The chrysalis closely resembles a bird dropping, an effective camouflage against predators such as birds. The adults are on the wing late in June and throughout most of July.

Black hairstreaks are not very active butterflies. Because they do not travel far, they have to be searched for and are seldom noticed by accident. (The reserve is in fact named for the person who first discovered these butterflies in Bernwood.)

Although blackthorn is common, both in and out of woodland, the butterfly is confined to the area lying generally between Oxford and Peterborough. It seems to prefer blackthorn growing thickly in sheltered but sunny places such as open woodland rides and clearings, and there are at least three BBONT grassland reserves with colonies in hedgerows.

Its rarity may in part be explained by its reluctance to fly far. It rarely colonises new sites, and so there is a risk to its survival in the event of its home thicket becoming unsuitable in some way. In the much more varied countryside of the past, blackthorn thickets of suitable age were quite likely to be within easy reach.

Management

To provide blackthorn of varied ages, some of the over-mature growth has been cut and removed so that young healthily suckering shoots can grow up. Oak and ash trees have also been felled because of the shade they cast on the young growth.

Burrows Reserve, Bernwood

OS sheet 164 & 165; SP 624114

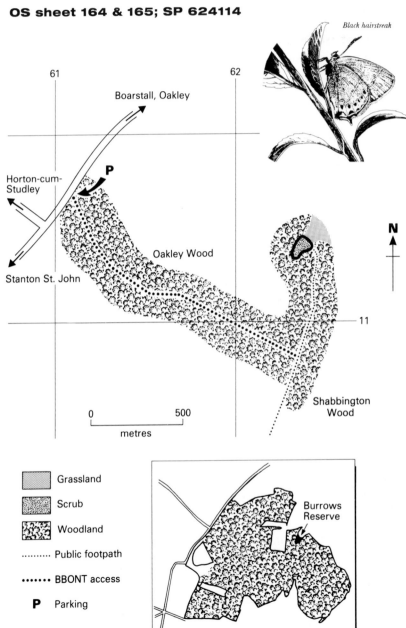

Black hairstreak

Boarstall, Oakley

P

Horton-cum-
Studley

Stanton St. John

Oakley Wood

N

11

0   500

metres

Shabbington
Wood

Grassland

Scrub

Woodland

.... Public footpath

•••••• BBONT access

P   Parking

Burrows
Reserve

Buttler's Hangings

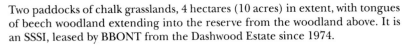

OS sheet 165; SU 818959

Nearest town High Wycombe

Two paddocks of chalk grasslands, 4 hectares (10 acres) in extent, with tongues of beech woodland extending into the reserve from the woodland above. It is an SSSI, leased by BBONT from the Dashwood Estate since 1974.

Location
Leave the A40 and West Wycombe via Chorley Road northwards to Bledlow Ridge and Chinnor. Where the road divides into three, park on the road verge and walk 300 metres along the right hand fork to where a public footpath crosses the road. Take the footpath going east. This leads to and crosses the reserve on the south-west facing slope of the valley and continues on into Hearnton Wood and Bradenham.

Access
The footpath is public access. The remainder of the reserve is open to BBONT members only.

Description
This chalk grassland reserve was ungrazed, except by rabbits, for over 20 years prior to BBONT's lease. Their grazing must have been light for the paddocks were invaded on the lower slopes by a scrub composed of hawthorn, dogwood and other shrubs. A good variety of wild flowers can be found, including pyramidal orchid which can be seen in early summer (it flowers 6–8) and the purplish flowered Chiltern gentian which appears later (8–9). Wild candytuft, a Chiltern speciality, flowers (7–8) at the top of the slope.

Invertebrates on the reserve have been studied for many years and 108 species of spider, including two national rarities, have been recorded. Twenty-five species of butterfly, out of a total of 34 recorded for the reserve, are regularly on the wing in the two paddocks. These include marbled whites (the caterpillars of which are grass feeders) and chalkhill blues, both of which do well on this warm sunny slope. In good years, clouded yellows and painted ladies may also be seen.

The great green bush-cricket, a species more usually found on the south coast, is resident here. They are also known as long-horned grasshoppers because of their long antennae or 'whiskers'. The noise they make is particularly penetrating and a feature of warm summer nights on the reserve.

Management
Current management aims to restrict any invasion of scrub and leave the grassland open to the sunshine. Sheep from the BBONT sheep flock now graze the reserve during the winter months. This has resulted in a noticeable improvement in the variety of grassland plants, particularly in the northern paddock.

Buttler's Hangings

OS sheet 165; SU 818959

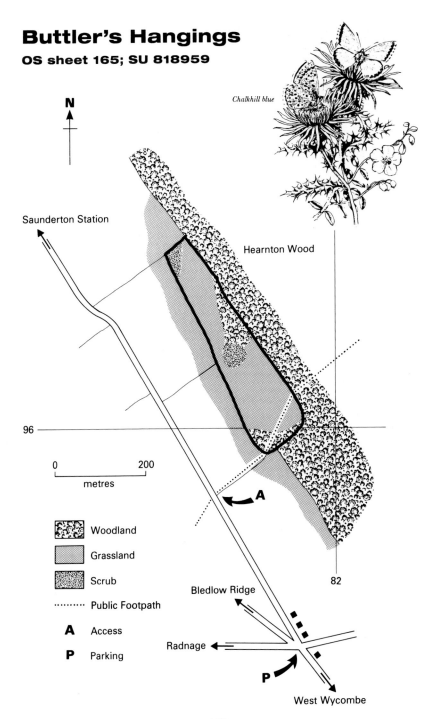

N

Saunderton Station

Hearnton Wood

Chalkhill blue

96

0 ____ 200
metres

Woodland

Grassland

Scrub

.... Public Footpath

A Access

P Parking

A

82

Bledlow Ridge

Radnage

West Wycombe

P

Cholsey Marsh

OS sheet 174/175; SU 601855

Nearest town Wallingford

An area of marsh, 11.9 hectares (29.4 acres) in area. It has been leased to BBONT since 1986.

Location
Leave Wallingford southwards on the A329, cross the Wallingford by-pass, and continue until reaching Fairmile Hospital on your left. At the crossroads beyond, turn sharp left and proceed slowly down Ferry Lane towards the River Thames. Park on the verge near the end of the lane. The reserve lies beside the Thames on both sides of Ferry Lane.

Access
Open to the public. Dogs should be kept on leads.

Description
At first sight a rather featureless area, this reserve is in fact full of interest. It is a relic of a type of habitat which was common along river systems but which has largely now been drained. Several rather different areas can be identified within it. One has little else but pond sedge growing. Another is marked by meadowsweet (flowering 6–9). The tassels of reed sweet-grass can be seen in places (6–8).

The Thames is a dominant feature through the entire length of the reserve, and in summer good numbers of riverine dragonfly species emerge and can easily be seen in their adult stage. Club-tailed dragonfly, banded demoiselle and white-legged damselfly are just three species to watch for.

The main interest of the reserve is its birds and it supplies the requirements for numerous different species along its length. The most obvious ones are along the River Thames itself, where species such as kingfisher, mute swan and great crested grebe can regularly be seen during the summer months.

Reed warbler, sedge warbler and reed bunting can be seen hunting among the reeds and willows while the occasional grasshopper warbler can be heard reeling deep within the vegetation. Snipe also breed here and their unusual 'drumming' display flight can be watched in spring and early summer.

Swallows congregate to roost here in late summer. Their sudden departure (which amazed people in the days before the secrets of migration were known) is a sign of impending autumn.

It is from late summer through to spring that the site really comes to life. Cholsey Marsh is a favoured winter roosting site for wagtails and reed buntings. Well over a hundred meadow pipits at a time are often seen and there are also large numbers of corn buntings regularly arriving to roost – the reserve is a winter stronghold for corn bunting in this part of Oxfordshire.

Management
Rubbish tipping has been stopped. The site has been fenced for cattle grazing and a pond has been dug thanks to the National Rivers Authority.

Cholsey Marsh

OS sheet 174/175; SU 601855

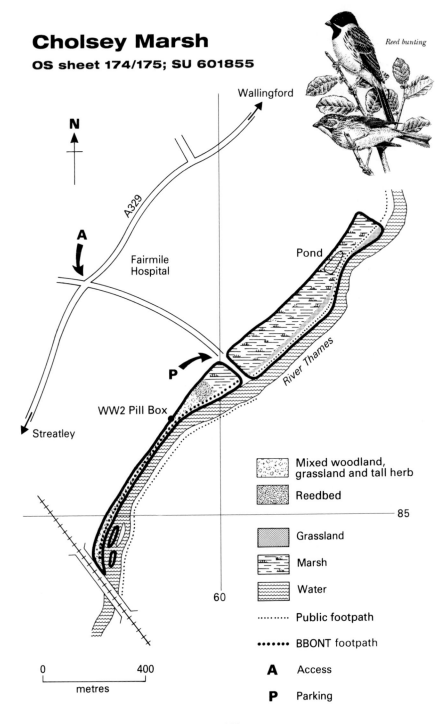

Reed bunting

Wallingford

N

A329

A

Fairmile
Hospital

Pond

River Thames

P

WW2 Pill Box

Streatley

Mixed woodland,
grassland and tall herb

Reedbed

85

Grassland

Marsh

Water

60

·········· Public footpath

•••••• BBONT footpath

A   Access

P   Parking

0   400
metres

Cowcroft

OS sheet 165; SP 986018

Nearest town Chesham

An area of grassland, scrub and woodland, 0.6 hectares (1.5 acres) in area. The freehold was given to BBONT by Messrs Harman (Cowcroft) Ltd in 1980.

Location

Leave Chesham on the unclassified road through Botley to the T-junction at Ley Hill. Turn right and park where indicated on the map. The reserve lies ¼ mile down the track, just before Cowcroft Wood.

Access

Open to the public.

Description

This area of grassland and scrub has an old brick pit on its south side and Cowcroft Wood on its west side. The site is on disturbed calcareous (chalky) soil, and supports a great variety of flowering plants. Altogether, over 160 species have been recorded, including common centaury (flowering 6–10), eyebright (7–8), common spotted-orchid (6–8) and bee orchid (6–7).

An orchid site is always worth visiting. The strange beauty of these wild flowers has attracted generations of nature lovers. It is interesting to speculate on possible reasons for why they are so abundant in some places and years but not others, even when the soil and other conditions seem to be very similar.

Wild orchids are plants with a fragile and complex lifestyle. They produce large amounts of very small dust-like seeds which are widely spread by the wind, and so there is a good chance of them reaching suitable soil. The majority of our orchids prefer a warm dry climate, many of them growing on southern chalk soils, and are more common in Europe than here.

Being small, their seeds carry little food reserves and growth is slow – it may be two or three years before the first small green leaf appears. In the meantime, the young orchid relies on the presence of a helpful soil fungus which invades the roots of the young plant. This fungus obtains nourishment from decaying matter in the soil and the orchid takes a share. It is thought that the orchid may not be able to colonise new ground without the presence of the fungus.

The bee orchid which can be seen here has additional interest. Its velvet-textured lip resembles the back of a bumble bee. The male bumble bees are misled into thinking the flower is a female bumble bee and try to mate with it, accidentally covering their bodies with pollen. They then fly to the next flower, again trying to mate. Pollen is transferred from the previous flower to this one, thus pollinating it.

Management

This consists mainly of keeping the scrub under control.

Cowcroft

OS sheet 165; SP 986018

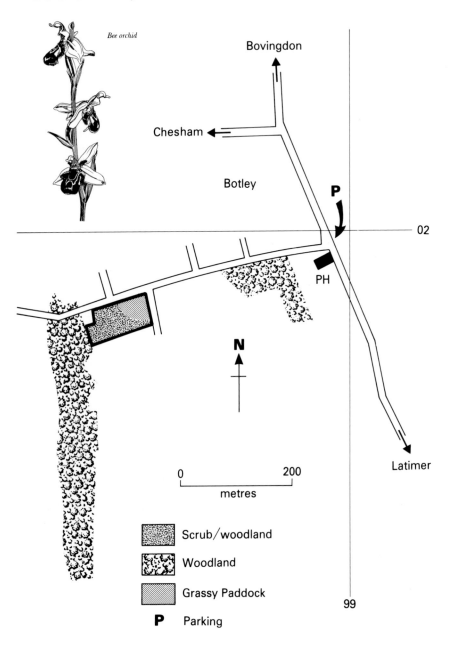

Bee orchid

Bovingdon

Chesham

Botley

P

02

PH

Latimer

N

0   200

metres

99

Scrub/woodland

Woodland

Grassy Paddock

P   Parking

111

Glyme Valley
OS sheet 164; SP 333260

Nearest town Chipping Norton

This BBONT reserve was leased from Thames Water in 1988. It forms a part of an SSSI and consists of 2.3 hectares (5.7 acres) of secluded valley, part of the headwater reaches of the River Glyme.

Location
Leave Chipping Norton directly east on the A44 London road. About ½ mile past the Parker Knoll factory at the edge of Chipping Norton (but before the golf course), there is a lay-by at SP 329274. Park here and walk down the public footpath (known locally as Swing-Swang Lane). This goes past New Chalford Farm on the way to the reserve. Alternatively, entry can be gained along the footpath from Chalford Green, SP 343246, where parking is available.

Access
Open to the public, but keep dogs under control if sheep are grazing.

Description
Although relatively small in area, the seclusion and variety of habitats of this reserve make for a delightful visit. The reserve consists of a south-facing slope running down to the River Glyme. Most of it is open limestone grassland scattered with small hawthorn bushes merging into denser scrub along the north and south edges. There is blackthorn and willow in places, and ash-dominated woodland in two corners. The southern stretch of dense scrub running along the River Glyme has enclosed one or two grassy glades.

The coarse look of the grassland and the encroachment of shrubs and trees are the results of the lack of regular grazing management for some years. Although ungrazed, luckily the grassland has not been agriculturally 'improved' by ploughing and reseeding or by the use of fertilizers and herbicides, so wild flowers are still present.

The variety of wild flowers on display and the large anthills suggest that this is also unploughed grassland. There is, for example, yellow rattle (flowering 5–8). It is an annual plant, parasitic on the roots of grasses, and typical of undisturbed grassland. The noise it makes as you walk through in autumn betrays its presence – its large seeds rattle inside the ripe seed pod, hence the name.

The wild flower list includes oxeye daisy (5–9), and the white fairy flax (6–9). Species such as cowslip (4–5) and salad burnet with round heads of greenish flowers (5–8) are indicators of the limey soil resulting from the rock below.

Management
Grazing and/or cutting the open grassland will maintain it and its flowers, while areas of scrub are cut from time to time to create blocks of varying age and structure. The glades in the southern length of scrub will be kept open.

Glyme Valley

OS sheet 164; SP 333260

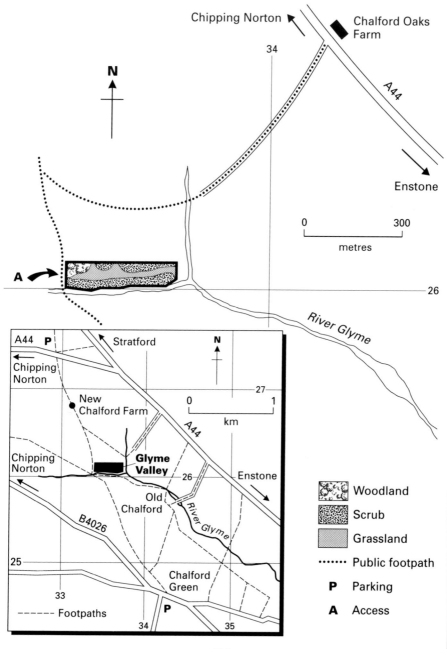

Chipping Norton

Chalford Oaks Farm

A44

Enstone

N

0   300
metres

26

River Glyme

A

A44   P

Stratford

N

Chipping Norton

New Chalford Farm

A44

0   1
km

27

Glyme Valley

Chipping Norton

26

Enstone

Old Chalford

River Glyme

B4026

25

Chalford Green

33

P

- - - - - Footpaths

34

35

Woodland

Scrub

Grassland

.... Public footpath

P   Parking

A   Access

OPEN ACCESS NATURE RESERVES

Gomm Valley

OS sheet 175; SU 896921

Nearest town High Wycombe

Previously open grassland, invaded by scrub, 4 hectares (10 acres) in extent. An SSSI, it has been managed by BBONT since 1969 by agreement with the owners.

Location

From the centre of High Wycombe take the A40 eastwards towards Beaconsfield for about 1½ miles, turn left up Gomm Road and park before or after the bridge. Take the public footpath diagonally across the slope to the first stile and then follow the lower path along the foot of the grassy slope and through the hedge into the next field. After 30 metres the path enters the reserve on the right.

Access

Open to the public.

Description

The history of the site is uncertain, but on the evidence of other dogwood scrub sites it was possibly once arable land. It is an excellent example of what has been called 'southern chalk scrub', being dominated by dogwood (flowering 5–7), and hawthorn (5–6), but with buckthorn (5–6), spindle, (5–6) guelder-rose (6–7) and wayfaring-tree (5–6). The wayfaring-tree is so called because John Gerard, a 16th century botanist, wrote that it was the most common shrub the wayfarer would encounter. The shrubs provide a good display of blossom in season followed by brightly coloured berries in the autumn. These attract many birds in winter, especially those of the thrush family.

Common spotted-orchid (flowering 6–8) and bee (6–7) and pyramidal (6–8) orchids grow in the grassy areas while common twayblades (6–7) flourish in the scrub margins.

In spring, bluebells (4–6) are found at the top of the mixed broad-leaved woodland at the southern end of the reserve. Here, also, are small patches of wood anemone (4–6) and the dainty coralroot with rose-pink flowers (4–5). The coralroot has a restricted range in Britain, being found mainly in parts of Kent and the Chilterns, particularly around High Wycombe. It rarely produces viable seeds and usually reproduces by means of little bulbils which develop in the leaf axils, fall off and grow into new plants.

The reserve is noted for its butterflies and has a thriving population of dark green fritillaries which are currently declining elsewhere in the country. Many marbled white butterflies can be seen on the reserve and on the grassy bank to the south of the reserve. Over 180 species of moth and 38 types of plant gall have been recorded. The reserve is also worth visiting around dusk when glow-worms can be seen. The wingless females of this species emit a cold greenish light to attract the winged males.

Management

The scrub must be kept under control; dogwood regenerates vigorously if cut in the winter and so summer cutting is to be adopted as part of the future management of this reserve.

Gomm Valley

OS sheet 175; SU 896921

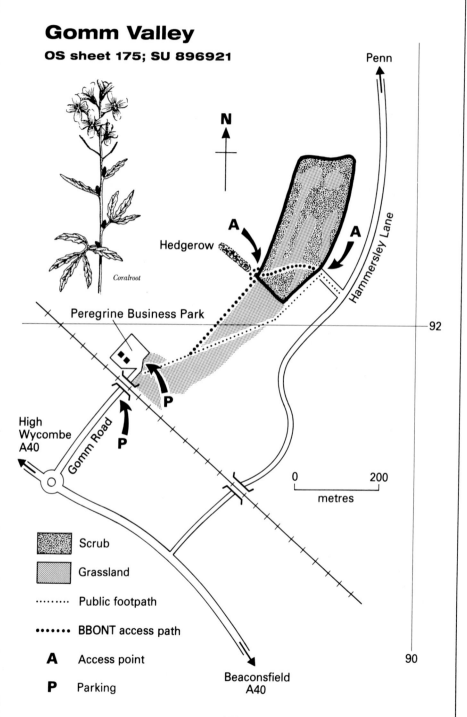

Coralroot

Penn

Hedgerow

N

A

A

Hammersley Lane

Peregrine Business Park

92

P

High
Wycombe
A40

Gomm Road

P

0   200

metres

Scrub

Grassland

········ Public footpath

•••••• BBONT access path

A Access point

P Parking

Beaconsfield
A40

90

Harry Williams'/Lamb's Pool Reserve

OS sheet 151; SP 353362

Nearest towns Chipping Norton and Banbury

A reserve of 2 hectares (5 acres). It was given to BBONT by Mr and Mrs J.A. Lamb of Sibford Ferris. It is also named in memory of Harry Williams who was a well-known and respected local naturalist and a voluntary reserve manager until his death in 1987.

Location

From Hook Norton, a village which lies to the north of the A361 between Chipping Norton and Banbury, take the unclassified road running north towards Sibford Ferris. Go straight ahead at the crossroads past the 'The Gate Hangs High' public house. Continue to the bottom of the hill and park on the left verge. Cross the stile and continue on foot along the left-hand hedge to where there is a gate into the reserve.

Access

Open to the public, but visitors are asked to respect plant and bird life and not to use the north bank during the nesting season from 1 February to 31 July. Please keep dogs on a lead.

Description

This is a man-made reservoir. It has a dam along the south side and western end, fed by water taken from the stream which forms the head of the River Stour. The rest of the reserve consists of a narrow strip of land around the reservoir.

Aquatic plants have been introduced and have successfully colonised the shallow (eastern) end of the reservoir. Here bur-reed now grows, easily recognised by its round spiky fruiting heads. Handsome yellow iris (flowering 5–7) and kingcup or marsh-marigold (3–5) are reserve wild flowers. Like many wetland species they are no longer so easy to find growing in the general countryside outside nature reserves. The bulrush also grows here, recognised by its brown sausage-like head. Until recently botanists called the plant, quite correctly, the greater reed mace. However, confusion arose in Victorian times with the painting of "Moses amongst the Bulrushes" by the artist Alma-Tadema. The artist painted reed mace and people mistakenly thought they must be bulrushes. To avoid future confusion, the greater reed mace has now officially been renamed the bulrush.

This reserve is now a fine place for birds – coot, moorhen, little grebe, mallard and tufted duck, mute swan and Canada goose have all nested around the open water and on the island. Nests of 19 other species have been recorded elsewhere on the reserve.

Management

The bank along the south side needs periodic attention to repair dilapidation caused by wind and wave action. Willows are pollarded and the eastern bank is mown to prevent colonisation by scrub.

Harry Williams'/Lamb's Pool Reserve

OS sheet 151; SP 353362

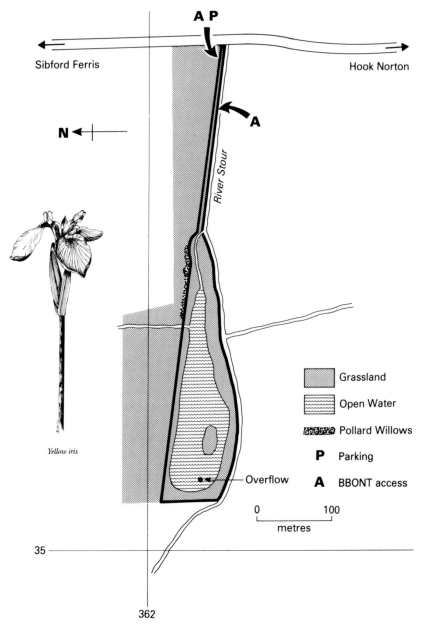

Sibford Ferris

Hook Norton

A P

N

River Stour

A

Yellow iris

Overflow

Grassland	
Open Water	
Pollard Willows	
P	Parking
A	BBONT access

0   100
metres

35

362

117

Hartslock

OS sheet 175; SU 616796

Nearest towns Goring and Streatley

An area of rich chalk grassland, 4.4 hectares (11 acres) in area. It is of SSSI status (part of a larger area of SSSI) bought by BBONT in 1975.

Location

Approaching Goring from the Oxford direction, take the A329 to Streatley. Turn left at the traffic lights, cross the river into Goring and straight on past the shops to a T-junction, where you turn right. Goring Station is ahead on the right.

Drive past the station for a mile and park off the road by the first or second junction. Walk up the right hand track to a gate on the right that leads to the reserve. This track must be kept clear as it is used by farm vehicles. If you prefer the exercise, it is not very far to walk from Goring to the reserve.

Access

Open to the public. Please keep dogs on a lead at all times when the BBONT sheep are grazing. Please do not cross the temporary fence lines which mark areas where research is being carried out, looking into such things as the effects of grazing.

Description

This reserve lies on steep slopes overlooking the Goring Gap, where the Thames cuts through the chalk downs.

From afar, the reserve is the characteristic tawny colour of old, traditionally grazed grassland, neither ploughed nor artificially fertilized. The hue, which can be seen from trains crossing the Thames on Brunel's bridge nearby comes from the rich variety of many wild grasses and wild flowers. Common rock-rose (flowering 5–9), harebell (7–9), bird's-foot-trefoil (6–9) and the uncommon bastard-toadflax (6–8) are among those growing here. The thin red stems of dodder (7–9) can also be seen. This plant is parasitic on other plants, and does not have roots of its own. Instead, it gains nourishment from the stems of the plants on which it grows.

The reserve is also home to a number of chalk downland butterflies, and several hundred moth species have been recorded.

Management

When BBONT acquired the site, scrub had begun to colonise. Although scrub can provide birds with secure nest sites, it does mean the loss of light-loving grassland flowers and consequently the butterflies and other insects reliant on them.

The quality of the grassland is now maintained by sheep grazing. Fences have been erected to carefully control where they graze. The effect of grazing at different times of year is monitored by the success or otherwise of the wild flowers and wildlife in the various compartments.

Hartslock

OS sheet 175; SU 616796

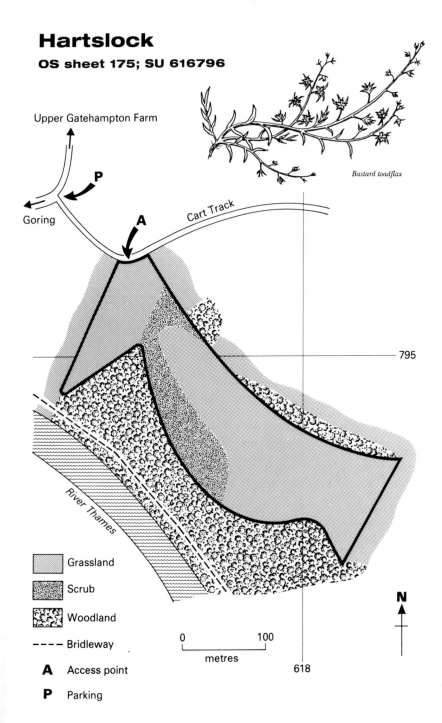

Upper Gatehampton Farm

P

Goring

Cart Track

A

Bastard toadflax

795

River Thames

Grassland

Scrub

Woodland

- - - - Bridleway

A Access point

P Parking

0   100

metres

618

N

Haymill Valley

OS sheet 175; SU 941820

Nearest town Slough

Haymill Valley, a 7.3 hectare (18 acre) site, which includes a silted-up mill pond, lies on the western edge of Slough Trading Estate. Mills have existed here since 1295, but the last was demolished in 1960. BBONT now has a 99 year lease on the site from Slough Borough Council, who have also provided an endowment for future management of the site.

Location

Leave the M4 at junction 7 and take the third exit at the roundabout for Slough along the A4. After ½ mile, turn left at Burnham Station and past this turn left at the junction with Burnham Lane. Go 450 metres and take the right fork opposite the Harvest public house into Haymill Road. At the mini-roundabout turn into Whittaker Road. The reserve starts at the junction of Whittaker Road with Littlebrook Avenue.

Access

Open to the public.

Description

Haymill Valley is one of the few wildlife havens within the urban area of Slough and is therefore of great importance. It consists mainly of mixed woodland around a large reedbed with small patches of grass and scrub.

The woodland in the reserve is made up mainly of willow, mixed with alder, elm and oak. This provides a variety of colours throughout the year, and a rich habitat for wildlife. In spring, bluebells (4–6) add a splash of colour to the woods. At this time, birds, including great spotted woodpeckers, nest in the trees above, while a variety of butterflies, including the orange-tip, brimstone and speckled wood, can be seen flying along the edge of the woodland.

With dense undergrowth deterring human disturbance, small animals such as hedgehogs, moles and slow-worms are present. Muntjac deer can often be seen browsing new tree shoots.

At the centre of the reserve lies the old mill pond with the stream flowing nearby. After the mill pond was abandoned, it slowly filled up with silt and developed into a reedbed. This is a particularly rare habitat due to land drainage and dropping water tables. Slough Estates, the owners of the nearby trading estate, sponsored the construction of three weirs which have saved the reedbed from drying up and even increased its size.

Colour is added to the reedbed by wetland wild flowers such as yellow iris (6–8) and marsh-marigold (3–5). The reeds give cover for nesting reed buntings and reed warblers and encourages mallard and coot to the small pond that remains at the edge of the reedbed close to the stream.

Management

Invading willow carr is removed to protect the reedbed, while mature willow pollards are re-pollarded to prevent them becoming dangerously unstable. Hazel is coppiced to create nesting sites for birds. A circular path is planned.

Haymill Valley

OS sheet 175; SU 941820

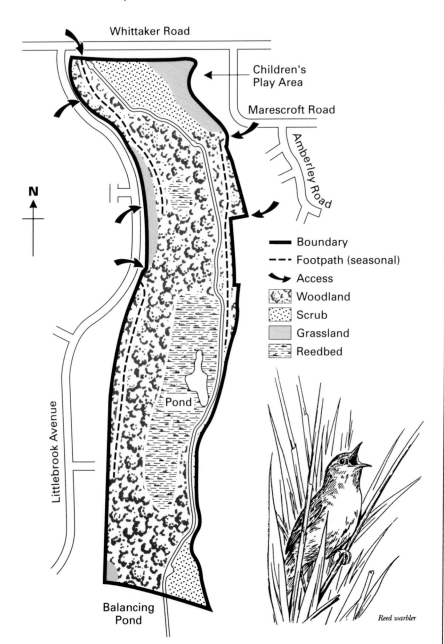

Whittaker Road

Children's Play Area

Marescroft Road

Amberley Road

N

Littlebrook Avenue

Pond

Balancing Pond

— Boundary
--- Footpath (seasonal)
↘ Access
Woodland
Scrub
Grassland
Reedbed

Reed warbler

121

Homefield Wood

OS Sheet 175; SU 814867

Nearest town Marlow

A 6 hectare (15 acre) site of young plantation woodland, occupying a south-facing slope, with areas of open grassland. It has been owned by the Forestry Commission since 1955, and managed by BBONT under agreement, since 1969. In 1984 it was notified as an SSSI.

Location

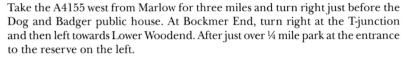

Take the A4155 west from Marlow for three miles and turn right just before the Dog and Badger public house. At Bockmer End, turn right at the T-junction and then left towards Lower Woodend. After just over ¼ mile park at the entrance to the reserve on the left.

Access

Open to the public along Forest Enterprise rides.

Description

From old maps of the area, it is known that woodland and grassland has existed here for at least 200 years. However, the once mature trees were clear felled in 1947, leaving only isolated larch and yew.

Most of Homefield Wood was replanted with conifers in the 1950s but beech trees were planted in the nature reserve area in 1960/61. A wide range of trees have since regenerated naturally. This has produced an interesting beech woodland, mixed with ash, sycamore and whitebeam among others, containing pleasant woodland glades and areas of thick undergrowth. Despite the presence of Dutch elm disease, wych elm supports the scarce white-letter hairstreak butterfly, and some young English elms survive here.

The open grassland is semi-natural, as it has probably not been ploughed or sprayed with chemicals for the past 200 years. This has created some rich chalk grassland habitat, with over 120 different plant species, and a smaller area of slightly less rich grassland habitat lying on clay.

In spring, these grasslands are covered by primroses (3–5) and violets (3–5). There are 11 types of orchids to be seen during the summer, including the common spotted-orchid (6–8) and the fly (5–6) and bee (6–7) orchids. Even in autumn the chalk grassland is colourful with displays of Chiltern gentian (7–9). The flower-rich grassland supports many butterflies, including marbled whites and common blues, and over 400 species of moth have been recorded.

Fallow, roe and muntjac deer are often seen and foxes are regular visitors. The presence of dormice was confirmed in 1993 and pipistrelle bats are frequently sighted in the evenings.

The visitor is always greeted by birdsong at the reserve, with 41 resident or visiting species. These include the chiffchaff, cuckoo, blackcap and tawny owl.

Management

Current management is designed to provide a range of habitat types, from woodland glades through light scrub to short chalk grassland turf. Sheep graze the grass areas in rotation, to maintain them for flowers and butterflies.

Homefield Wood

OS Sheet 175; SU 814867

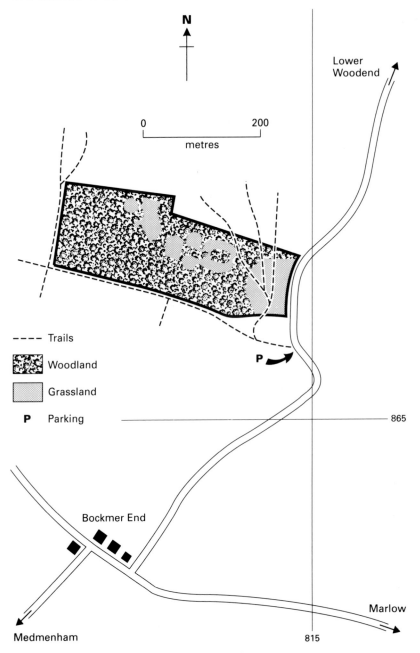

N

0   200
metres

Lower
Woodend

- - - - Trails

Woodland

Grassland

P   Parking

865

Bockmer End

Marlow

Medmenham

815

Hook Norton Railway Cutting
OS sheet 151; SP 360322

Nearest towns Banbury and Chipping Norton

A length of disused railway line, totalling 7.7 hectares (19 acres). All but the part north of the road bridge at SP 360323 is an SSSI, scheduled mainly for its geological interest. The site was bought by BBONT in 1972.

Location
From Banbury take the A361 towards Chipping Norton. About 2 miles after South Newington turn right along the unclassified road through Swerford and towards Hook Norton. After 1 mile, fork right. Cross the railway bridge and park in the lay-by on the right. Access to the reserve is on the other side of the bridge.

To reach the southern section, continue in the direction of Hook Norton, then turn sharp left. At the T-junction turn right, and then left after 50 metres. Park down the hill by the remains of the railway bridge. Access is by the stile on the left.

Access
Open to the public. The railway line was used to transport iron ore from the Hook Norton area to blast furnaces in the Midlands and South Wales. It was closed in 1963 after quarrying ceased. The tunnel separating the two sections does not belong to BBONT and is out of bounds.

Description
The geological interest lies in the exposed Jurassic oolitic limestones, which have been used in house and stone walls in the area. The stones are stained red due to the presence of iron oxide.

Three main areas can be recognised. North of the road bridge, on the embankment, there is a developing woodland of oak and maple to the west and a mixture of scrub and woodland to the east. The centre section is also developing woodland, here dominated by ash and willows. Male fern and hart's-tongue fern are also to be seen here.

In spring and summer these areas are alive with bird song. Among the 47 recorded species, those nesting include woodpeckers (great spotted and green), garden warblers, blackcaps, whitethroats and goldcrests. For the specialist, the retaining walls along the track have many different lichens.

The southern section provides what is essentially limestone grassland with encroaching scrub. Amongst the many wild flowers, kidney vetch (flowering 6–9) and wild carrot (6–8) are abundant.

Butterflies, including marbled whites, are numerous. The cutting is particularly notable for its populations of bees.

Management
On the northern sections the vegetation on each side of the railway track is cut in alternate years. Much of the invasive scrub has been removed from the southern section, which is grazed by sheep.

Hook Norton Railway Cutting

OS sheet 151; SP 360322

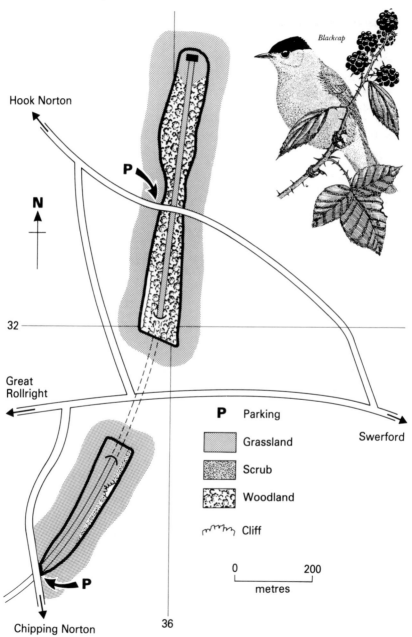

Blackcap

Hook Norton

N

Great Rollright

32

Swerford

P Parking

Grassland

Scrub

Woodland

Cliff

0   200
metres

Chipping Norton

36

Horley

OS sheet 151; SP 407428

Nearest town Banbury

An old railway line, siding and quarry workings, 12 hectares (30 acres) in area. BBONT has leased it since 1982.

Location

From Banbury take the B4100 north and then fork left at the traffic lights along the A422 towards Stratford-upon-Avon. Continue to Wroxton and take the third turn on the right on the western outskirts along an unclassified road. Parking is after the first turning on the right (a staggered junction) as shown on the map.

Access

Open to the public.

Description

The reserve consists of an old railway line and siding with old ironstone quarry workings alongside. When the railway line was abandoned, the natural process of succession began and scrub started to invade.

There are a variety of habitats. Areas of dense scrub are beginning to develop into woodland on some of the steep banks. Scrub species such as hawthorn and blackthorn (sloe) have seeds which are easily spread by birds. The seeds germinate and the seedlings develop to form a dense cover. Shaded as they are, the growth of the tree saplings may be slow at first but the scrub protects them from rabbits and other grazing animals. Succession can be swift. In the space of 60 years, bare stretches of ground have become tall woodland.

The reserve also has two larch plantations. Larch foliage lets quite a bit of light through so larch woods often contain other woody species. Here we have hazel, elder and holly as well as some grey alder.

The short grassy bank and track and the flat grassy area have many wild flowers. Although there are no very unusual plants, cover is provided for mice, voles and shrews as well as for some birds.

In all, 170 different plant species have been recorded at Horley, 43 species of breeding birds, and 11 of butterflies, including the marbled white.

Management

Some scrub control is undertaken to maintain the areas of open grassland. Ideally this should now be grazed, preferably by sheep. From a conservation point of view sheep are easier to manage (especially on a mixed site such as this) and rather more beneficial than cattle. With the correct stocking rates, sheep can produce a fine sward which encourages the growth of the shorter wild flowers. Cattle tend to tear wholesale at the plants but avoid cowpats (the site of which become marked by thistles) and their weight 'poaches' wet ground, turning it into a muddy morass.

Horley

OS sheet 151; SP 407428

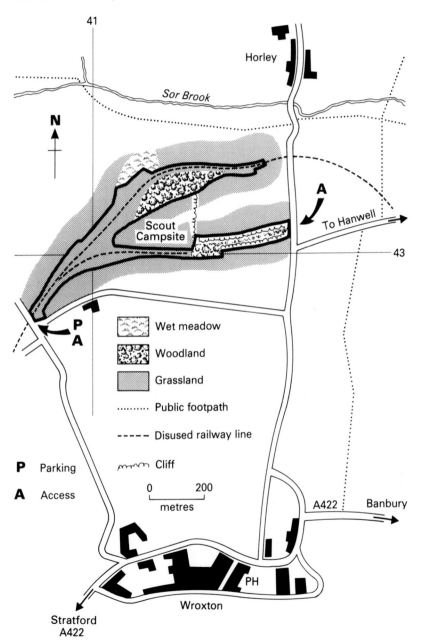

Wet meadow
Woodland
Grassland
Public footpath
Disused railway line
Cliff

P Parking

A Access

0   200
metres

Hornton Meadows
OS sheet 151; SP 395465

Nearest town Banbury

A pair of ancient meadows and an ancient hedgerow covering 6 hectares (15 acres) in all; bought by BBONT in 1988.

Location
Take the B4100 north from Banbury. Turn left towards Horley after 1½ miles (second left turn after the roundabout). In Horley, turn right at the T-junction and follow the road up the hill past a church on the left and continue for just over a mile. On the right is a bridleway just before a set of crossroads. Walk down the bridleway as shown on the map, and then walk along the boundary of the field to the reserve.

Access
Open to the public.

Description
The reserve lies in a valley and consists of two damp hay meadows surrounded by old hedgerows which contain a variety of different species of woody shrubs.

The number of shrubs can very often be used to give us an idea of the age of the hedgerow. It is marked into 30 yard lengths and a count is made of the number of different species in each length. Count all wild roses as one and ignore climbers. The average number per 30 yards is the age of the hedge in centuries. Hedgerow history can be complicated however, and not all hedges lend themselves to this handy method – for example, those hedges which were originally strips of woodland left when fields were cleared at each side rather than specifically planted as a barrier.

The two meadows are flower-rich. There is a abundance of great burnet (flowering (6–9), whose distinctive dull crimson cylindrical flower heads are a good 'indicator' of old unimproved meadows of this kind, and pignut (flowering 5–6), its underground tubers being the 'nuts in May' of the familiar children's rhyme.

Large numbers of frogs are to be found here in the spring. Our countryside was formerly dotted with ponds and pools. However, field ponds are usually filled when agricultural 'improvement' takes place and this, together with the general drainage of marshy areas, has caused even the 'common' frog to become less than common in today's countryside. We can no longer take frog spawn for granted.

The reserve is also notable for dragonflies and damselflies. Birds recorded as nesting in the hedges include the tree pipit.

Management
The reserve is being grazed by cattle.

Hornton Meadows

OS sheet 151; SP 395465

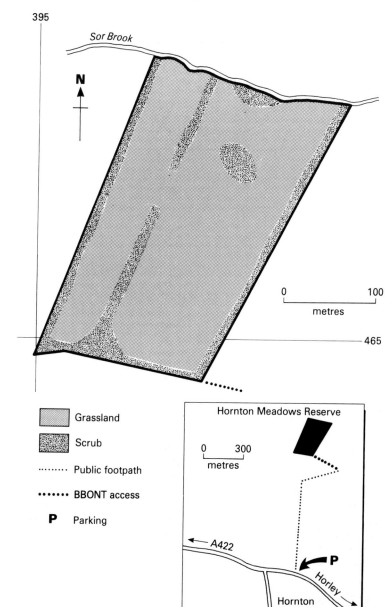

395

Sor Brook

N

0   100
metres

465

	Grassland
	Scrub
....	Public footpath
••••••	BBONT access
P	Parking

Hornton Meadows Reserve

0   300
metres

A422

P

Horley

Hornton

129

Hungerford Marsh

OS sheet 174; SU 333687

Nearest town Hungerford

Unimproved rough grazing and reedbed, 11.2 hectares (28 acres) in area. Both the reserve and the adjoining Freeman's Marsh form part of an SSSI. The reserve is managed by BBONT in agreement with the owner.

Location

The reserve is on the western edge of Hungerford, lying alongside the Kennet and Avon Canal, with the River Dun winding through it. From the centre of town go along Church Street, past the town hall and turn right under the railway. Follow the public footpath which crosses the canal via a swing bridge near the church. A line of willows and bushes on the western boundary separates it from Freeman's Marsh, managed by the Town and Manor of Hungerford.

Access

Open to the public (but please keep to the footpath).

Description

The River Dun flows across peaty ground which in the past was wetland. Today, the reserve consists of rough grass with some reedbed and alder woodland areas.

Colourful wetland wild flowers are still seen, including yellow iris (flowers 5–7) and ragged-Robin (5–6). There are southern marsh-orchids (6–7) and local fen bedstraw (6–8). When in flower (3–5) the handsome yellow marsh-marigold or kingcup can be seen from afar. It was a familiar plant in our grandparents' day, but with the wide scale field drainage and 'improvement' of recent times we can no longer take it for granted.

Several species of birds nest along the river banks and on the marshy meadows. Reed warblers nest in the reedbeds, sedge warblers across the entire reserve. The former expertly weaves a deep nest slung between the reed stems. Both are more frequently heard than seen in this dense cover, their songs having characteristic liquid and grating notes.

Snipe used to nest regularly on the reserve, and it is hoped that the current management will encourage them to do so again. The reserve would be well worth visiting just to witness their courtship display, when the cock bird climbs quite high with rapidly beating wings, then dives with its outer tail feathers spread. These vibrate in the slipstream to create a resonant bleating note or 'drumming'.

There are records of 120 different bird species over the last ten years or so, including heron, kingfisher, yellow wagtail, water rail, little grebe, mute swan and grasshopper warbler. The latter may nest here – its unusual song is a repetitive high-pitched machine-like whir delivered from deep cover. Siskins are frequent visitors to the alders. There are also moles, water voles and sometimes grass snakes on the reserve.

Management

The area to the south of the river is grazed by cattle from July to December. The area to the north is not grazed at all, allowing the reedbed to expand. The willows are pollarded at intervals.

Hungerford Marsh

OS sheet 174; SU 333687

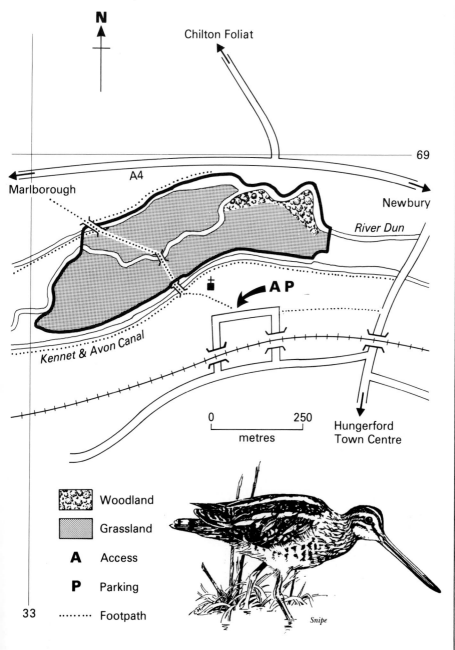

N

Chilton Foliat

Marlborough

A4

69

Newbury

River Dun

A P

Kennet & Avon Canal

0   250
metres

Hungerford
Town Centre

Woodland

Grassland

A   Access

P   Parking

.... Footpath

Snipe

33

Hurley Chalk Pit
OS sheet 175; SU 813822

Nearest town Henley-on-Thames

A small beech wood, chalk pit and an area of chalk grassland, 1.4 hectares (3.5 acres) in area. The freehold was bought by BBONT in 1964. It was BBONT's first acquisition by purchase.

Location

The reserve is reached on the A4130 from Henley to Maidenhead. Three miles from Henley, there is a lay-by on the left side of the road just before the Black Boy Inn (SU 812830). Visitors should park here. Follow the bridleway directly opposite the Inn for about a mile to the top of the rise and you will see the nature reserve sign.

Access

Open to the public. Please do not go near the unstable cliff edges or collect the fossils.

Description

Despite its name, only a part of this reserve is a chalk pit. The pit lies in the south-west corner and has chalk cliffs and scree. Flints and fossils are on open view.

Most of the reserve – just under 1 hectare of the total area – is beech wood mixed with oak, ash, field maple, wild cherry, crab apple, whitebeam and silver birch. The ground below the beech is mainly bare but during the spring has dog's mercury (2–5), violets and bluebells (4–6). During the summer months there is yellow archangel (5–6), wood avens (5–9), sanicle (5–7) and wood melick (5–6) as well as a few white helleborines (5–7).

Close by the pit is a small area of open chalk grassland with over 100 recorded plant species. These include rock-rose (5–9), wild thyme (6–9), clustered bellflower (6–10), carline thistle (7–9), dwarf thistle (6–9), glaucous sedge (5–6) and quaking-grass (6–8).

There are small numbers of wild orchids around the reserve, the most common being the pyramidal (6–8). In most years a few common spotted-orchid (6–8) and fragrant (6–7) and bee (6–7) orchids can also be seen.

The chalk pit itself has many of these wild flowers but is best known for its spring display of cowslips (4–5) and its wild candytuft (5–9) which grow on the scree. The west-facing pit is sheltered by the surrounding trees and appears to warm up quickly, making it a good place for butterflies. It attracts no fewer than 20 species including common blue, meadow brown, gatekeeper, brimstone and large and small skippers. However, from May to September the speckled wood is the most common species.

Management

Scrub is regularly cut back to keep the chalk pit and grassland open. The grassland is cut and raked in the autumn. Hazel in the woodland is coppiced about once every 10 years.

Hurley Chalk Pit

OS sheet 175; SU 813822

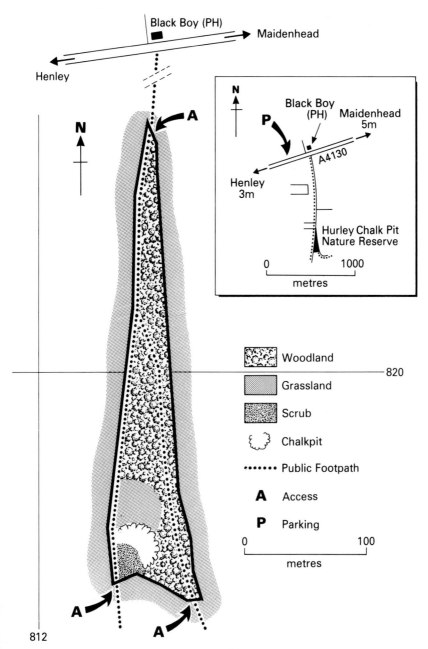

Black Boy (PH)

Maidenhead

Henley

N

A

N

Black Boy (PH)

Maidenhead 5m

P

A4130

Henley 3m

Hurley Chalk Pit Nature Reserve

0   1000
metres

820

Woodland

Grassland

Scrub

Chalkpit

•••••• Public Footpath

A Access

P Parking

0   100
metres

A

A

812

Iffley Meadows

OS sheet 164; SP 525036

Nearest town Oxford

Ancient wet meadow land, 33 hectare (82 acres), famous for its snake's-head fritillary flowers. An SSSI leased from Oxford City Council since 1983.

Location

The reserve may be reached by parking within Iffley Village and crossing the Thames via the bridge and lock gates at Iffley Lock, then turning right along the tow-path. The reserve is just past the Isis public house. (It is worth making a detour in the village to see the Norman carvings of Iffley Church.)

Alternatively, before reaching Iffley village from central Oxford turn right at traffic lights into Donnington Bridge Road. Park off this road in Meadow Lane before the bridge if possible. Walk across the bridge and along the tow-path to the entrance.

Access

Open to the public. Please take care not to trample the snake's-head fritillaries, especially when they are in flower. Dogs must be kept on a lead.

Description

The main interest of these ancient wet meadows, bordered by the River Thames, is the presence of the snake's-head fritillary, which flowers in late spring (4–5). It used to flower profusely across the meadows, but is now seen mainly around the centre of the section north of the ring road. Numbers were dropping before BBONT assumed control, not only as a result of picking but also from the lack of appropriate management. The numbers are now increasing. These meadows are one of the few remaining places in Britain where this plant can be seen flowering in its natural surroundings (rather than in gardens or garden centres).

The meadows are crossed by old river channels and willow-lined ditches. Much of the area has clay soil which is still enriched each year by silt brought by flooding. The meadows also have a wide variety of plants, many typical of old meadow land undamaged by farming improvements. These include adder's-tongue, great burnet (flowering 6–9), common meadow-rue (7–8), pepper-saxifrage (6–8), and creeping-Jenny (6–8).

Parts of the meadow are covered by deposits of gravel which makes the soil more acidic and so fewer wild flowers are seen here. However, plants such as meadow buttercup (flowering 5–8), ragged-Robin (5–6) and oxeye daisy (5–9) are fairly abundant everywhere. Marsh-marigold can also be seen in spring (3–5).

The field south of the ring road is wetter and more marshy than the rest of the reserve. Here meadowsweet can be seen flowering (6–9) alongside abundant soft rush.

Management

The meadows are mown in July after the seed from the fritillary plants has ripened. The hay is baled and removed and livestock are put on to graze the regrowth until November. The field south of the by-pass is managed as pasture and left uncut.

Iffley Meadows

OS sheet 164; SP 525036

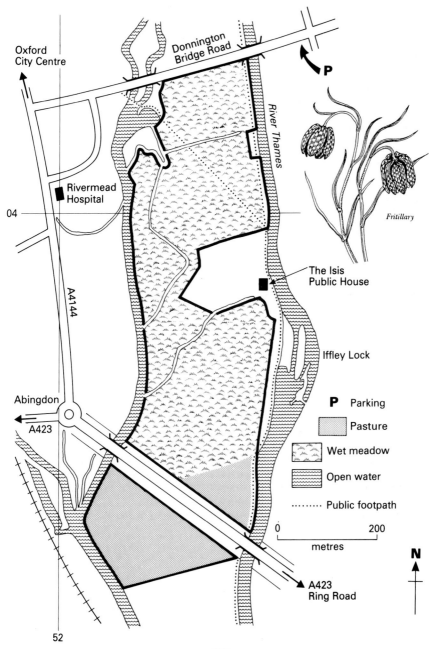

Fritillary

Oxford City Centre

Donnington Bridge Road

River Thames

P

Rivermead Hospital

04

A4144

The Isis Public House

Iffley Lock

Abingdon

A423

P Parking

Pasture

Wet meadow

Open water

········ Public footpath

0   200

metres

A423 Ring Road

N

52

135

Inkpen Crocus Field

OS sheet 174; SU 370640

Nearest town Hungerford

A thickly-hedged, flower-rich meadow site, notable for its wild crocuses. This SSSI is 3.2 hectares (8 acres) in area, and was bought by BBONT in 1986.

Location
From the A4, 3½ miles east of Hungerford, take the road leading south to Kintbury. Take the second left in Kintbury village, for Inkpen. After 1 mile turn right at the crossroads, and fork left after ½ mile. After a further ½ mile turn right onto a narrow concrete track (Pottery Lane). After 200 metres there is a grass track on the left with a gate at the end leading into Crocus Field.

Access
Open to the public. Dogs must be kept on a lead.

Description
This reserve boasts the largest population of spring crocuses in Britain, thousands of the purple or white-purple flowers being seen in March–April.

The spring crocus is not a native species. How it came to be here in Britain is a puzzle. Tradition has it that the plant was originally brought back by the Crusaders as a source of saffron for flavouring and colouring sweetmeats. However, this particular crocus does not produce saffron. Even more of a mystery is why there should be so many plants on this particular site. Records show that the flowers have been here since 1800 and farmers delayed grazing to protect them! One possible explanation is that it came with garden rubbish dumped long ago on the site – parts have been dug for clay at some time in the past and these diggings may have been used as a local waste tip. However, no one really knows.

Crocuses apart, these two fields separated by a small, spring-fed stream are fine examples of flower-rich meadow land on clay soil. The character of the undisturbed soil is reflected by the plants found. The northern meadow is particularly rich in wild grasses and wild flowers (and has more crocuses), while the southern has tougher grasses, fewer flowering plants and, in the wetter parts, rushes. Some 149 plant species have so far been recorded on the reserve, some of which are found only in 'unimproved' grassland such as this. One species of interest is pignut – a rather short relative of cow parsley. It grows from underground tubers and is seen in flower in May and June. These tubers are the 'nuts in May' gathered in the children's nursery rhyme.

With such a galaxy of wild flowers, a large variety of butterflies can be found including small and common blues.

Management
In the past grazing was intermittent. Horses were kept at times. It is now grazed by cattle.

Inkpen Crocus Field

OS sheet 174; SU 370640

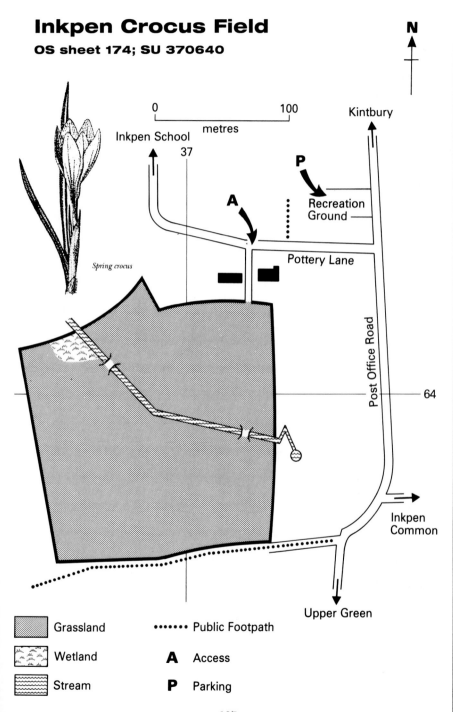

Spring crocus

Inkpen School

37

Kintbury

P

Recreation Ground

A

Pottery Lane

Post Office Road

64

Inkpen Common

Upper Green

0 — 100
metres

N

▓ Grassland	●●●●●● Public Footpath
Wetland	**A** Access
Stream	**P** Parking

137

Long Grove Wood
OS sheet 175; SU 961915

Nearest towns Beaconsfield and Amersham

A fragment of old mixed deciduous woodland, 1.6 hectares (4 acres) in area. BBONT was given the freehold in 1964. Long Grove Wood was one of BBONT's earliest reserves.

Location
From the roundabout at the junction of the A40 and A355 in Beaconsfield, take the A355 north for Amersham. After about 1 mile, take the right turn (Long Bottom Lane) to Seer Green and Chalfont St Peter. Take the second left along this road (School Lane) into Seer Green and then take the first left after the school (Stable Lane). Turn left at the end into Farmer's Way and park at the end. The public footpath from here enters and crosses Long Grove Wood in a south-west direction.

Access
Open to the public.

Description
This is a remaining piece of the old mixed deciduous woodland which once covered much of the Chilterns. The soil here is relatively poor – clay-with-flints interspersed with areas of gravel. The woodland contains a mixture of oak, beech, hornbeam, field maple and birch. Wild cherry is typically found in this type of woodland, but here there is only a solitary cherry tree. Ancient and gnarled coppice stools testify to prolonged coppicing of the beech in the past, but some of these stools have died in recent years and a number have become inactive through lack of light. The opening up of parts of the wood has also resulted in the appearance of many rowan saplings.

The Great Storm of October 1987 brought several trees to the ground, creating glades and benefiting woodland flowers including bluebell (flowering 4–6) and yellow archangel (5–6). Common cow-wheat (5–9) is worth looking out for – it is partially parasitic on other plants and is an indicator of old woodland.

It is interesting to see these old beech coppice stools in a wood of this kind. Beech is known for creating its own tall, clean-trunked woodland (the inspiration for the architecture of Gothic cathedrals, some believe). However on poorer soils it tends to become rather ungainly and, its timber value lost, it is often coppiced as here or pollarded (cut at head height) as at the famous Burnham Beeches.

Management
Although managed as coppice in the distant past, there will be limited management so that trees will be allowed to grow old, natural glades will be created when trees blow over and dead wood will be retained wherever possible.

Long Grove Wood

OS sheet 175; SU 961915

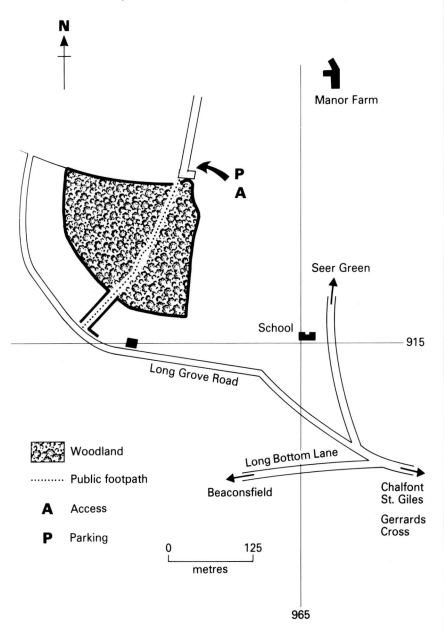

Manor Farm

N

P
A

Seer Green

School

915

Long Grove Road

Long Bottom Lane

Beaconsfield

Chalfont
St. Giles

Gerrards
Cross

965

Woodland

.... Public footpath

A Access

P Parking

0   125

metres

Long Herdon & Grange Meadows

OS sheet 165; SP 648203

Nearest town Bicester

A remnant of ancient meadow land, 10 hectares (25 acres) in extent. Long Herdon Meadow (5 hectares) is an SSSI, and was bought by BBONT in 1981. Grange Meadow was acquired by Plantlife in 1991 and is managed by BBONT.

Location

Leave Bicester on the A41 towards Aylesbury and take the second road, signposted to Marsh Gibbon. After ¾ mile, park on the verge just past Grange Farm. Enter through the gate and walk down the right-hand hedge to the reserve, which comprises the last four fields before the River Ray.

Access

Open to the public.

Description

These four fields represent a relic of traditional farming techniques. In the past, hay was an essential crop, keeping the horses and other livestock throughout the winter when the grass was unavailable. Each village had its hay meadows. They were often along streams due to grass growing better on damp soil. In recent decades over 90% of such meadows have been 'improved', artificially fertilized for better growth or drained and ploughed for cereals or rye grass.

There is evidence of past ploughing in the two smaller meadows. The visible ridge and furrow here is a result of pre-enclosure (1846) ploughing down to the flood line. The two main meadows have never been ploughed and are true flood meadows, being periodically flooded at any time of the year.

The fields have a rich collection of grasses, sedges, and flowers such as meadow thistle (flowering 6–8), common meadow-rue (7–8) and great burnet (6–9) and there is plentiful invertebrate life. Snipe and other birds typical of flood meadows might be expected to breed here.

Wet meadows, such as this, are important for bird life all year round. The reserve lies within the area encompassing the headwaters of the River Ray, an area which still holds large wintering flocks of waders such as lapwings. In common with many other species, however, they respond to the weather and in bleak and freezing times will make quite lengthy journeys to find suitable feeding grounds. They have delicate bills and feed by probing for worms and other invertebrates. This means that they need the soft unfrozen soil of wet meadows. In hard spells, flocks will move even further to the milder south or south-west.

At Long Herdon flocks of golden plover can be seen. Our British resident birds breed on the moors but come to lowland feeding grounds such as this in winter. However, golden plovers from Iceland and Scandinavia may also be seen.

Management

The meadows are cut for hay late in the season and the regrowth is grazed by cattle.

Long Herdon & Grange Meadows

OS sheet 165; SP 648203

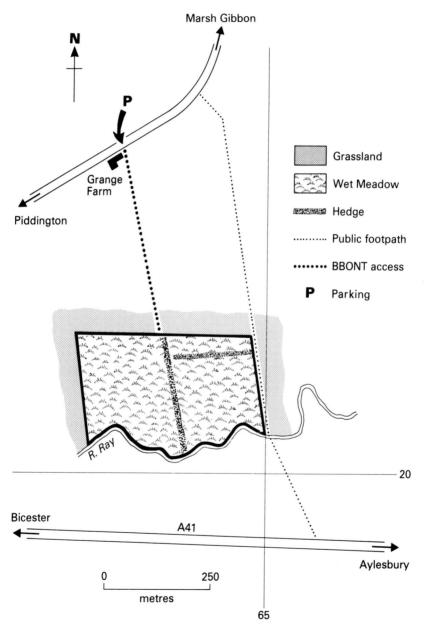

Marsh Gibbon

N

P

Grange Farm

Piddington

Grassland

Wet Meadow

Hedge

.... Public footpath

•••••••• BBONT access

P Parking

R. Ray

20

Bicester

A41

Aylesbury

0   250

metres

65

141

Millfield Wood

OS sheet 165; SU 870954

Nearest town High Wycombe

An example of a Chiltern beech wood, growing on chalk, totalling 7.3 hectares (19 acres). It is an SSSI, bought by BBONT in 1983.

Location
Take the A4128 from High Wycombe up the Hughenden Valley and turn left up the drive to Hughenden Manor. Park in the car park near the church and walk back down the drive. Cross the road to the bridleway opposite. Go up the hill, and the reserve can be found on the right. Take care crossing the busy A4128.

Access
Open to the public. There is a public footpath through the reserve.

Description

This is a rare example of a semi-natural Chiltern wood growing on chalk – an open 'high forest' with tall trees, mainly beech but with some ash and wild cherry. There is, at a lower level, a rather open 'understorey' of coppiced hazel, holly and field maple, and (towards the lighter edges of the wood) whitebeam.

Normally the floor of a beech wood is rather bare in spring, but here we can find a number of flowers. Many of them are typical of ancient woodland. Examples include the goldilocks buttercup (flowering 4–6) and wood anemone (4–6). Herb-Paris (5–7) is a plant worth looking out for, its leaves held in a hand of four at the top the stem. Lily-of-the-valley flowers here (5–6) – although often found in gardens, it is actually a native wild flower. There are also bluebells (4–6) and a scattering of sanicle (5–8).

Many birds live in the wood. Listen out for the chiffchaff between late May and July. Muntjac deer are also present.

After the last Ice Age, trees from Europe (of which Britain was still part) began to invade, creating a wildwood. Beech was the last to arrive before Britain split from the mainland and is therefore the last of our 'native' trees. It can outgrow and shade out the oak. However, Britain is on the fringe of its natural range and it cannot produce viable seed much further north. It is thought that beech trees north of Derby are probably all planted artificially as a source of timber.

Buckinghamshire could well have gained its name from natural woodlands of beech – the Old English name of this tree was 'bece', which easily becomes 'buck'

Timber was almost certainly extracted from this wood in the past. Nevertheless it now has a natural aspect – hence the description 'semi-natural'. The wood suffered severe damage in the 1990 storm but is recovering, with many more open areas than before and noticeable changes in the types of plants and animals.

Management
Clearing and maintaining the footpaths, removal of sycamore, horse chestnut and other invasive species and creation of open clearings to encourage the wild flowers and butterflies.

Millfield Wood

OS sheet 165; SU 870954

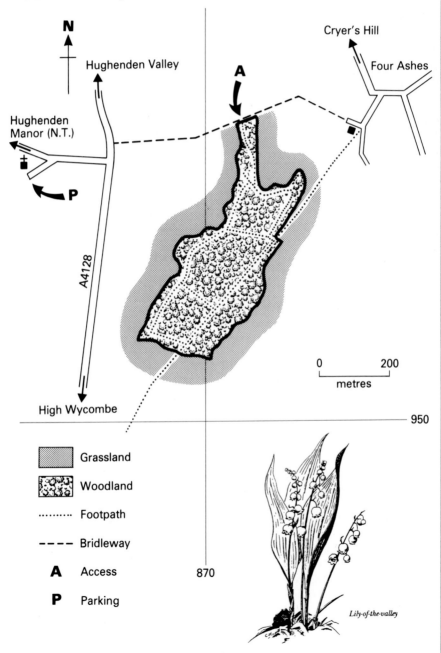

N

Hughenden Valley

Cryer's Hill

Four Ashes

A

Hughenden
Manor (N.T.)

P

A4128

High Wycombe

0   200
metres

950

870

Grassland

Woodland

.... Footpath

---- Bridleway

A   Access

P   Parking

Lily-of-the-valley

Northerams Wood
OS sheet 175; SU 856681

Nearest town Bracknell

A 3 hectare (7.5 acre) relic of an old woodland. It was leased to BBONT by Bracknell District Council, and declared a nature reserve in 1980.

Location
This is an urban reserve within Bracknell, adjoining the A3095, the main road from Bracknell to Crowthorne. The map opposite explains the route from this main road (Mill Lane). At the roundabout take the road to the west signposted Great Hollands, and follow it round to the right until you reach a car park on the right-hand side. Park here and walk across the playing fields to the reserve.

Access
Open to the public.

Description
This wood was saved by the action of local residents. A remnant of a much larger area of woodland, now largely built over with factories, it is valuable for being a wildlife-rich site within a built-up area.

It is mixed woodland with small areas of open damp meadow and some scrub. Within the woodland there are three kinds of habitat. Firstly oak scrub, secondly hazel coppice with birch, and thirdly a mixture of hazel, birch, sycamore, sweet chestnut, alder, aspen, holly, elder, wild cherry and hawthorn. It is surprisingly diverse for its size. More than 100 plant species have been recorded here, and there is a variety of wild flowers in spring including bluebell (flowering 4–6), and yellow archangel (5–6).

Eighteen different species of butterflies have been recorded including the white admiral and the brimstone. The latter, the familiar yellow butterfly of spring, may have given the 'butterfly' its name. The females (which are in fact not yellow but almost white) search for buckthorn bushes on which to lay their eggs. Many other species however are more common in the open areas of the wood. The small copper, common blue, meadow brown, small heath and other brown butterflies are all linked with grassy areas. The painted lady, a migrant butterfly from North Africa and Europe, has also been recorded here.

The birds recorded as nesting include blackcaps and garden and willow warblers, while woodpeckers have been heard drumming against the trees.

Management
The hazel in the woods is coppiced on a 15–20 year rotation system. This opens up the woodland floor to light, encouraging the wild flowers (and butterflies) and creating varied habitats for birds. Invasive sycamore is gradually being removed. The grassy areas are now mown each year to increase the diversity of the plants and the insects and other invertebrates which depend on them (mowing or grazing regimes tend to keep taller, coarse plants at bay and encourage the slighter wild flowers). A small pond has been dug in the grassland area.

Northerams Wood

OS sheet 175; SU 856681

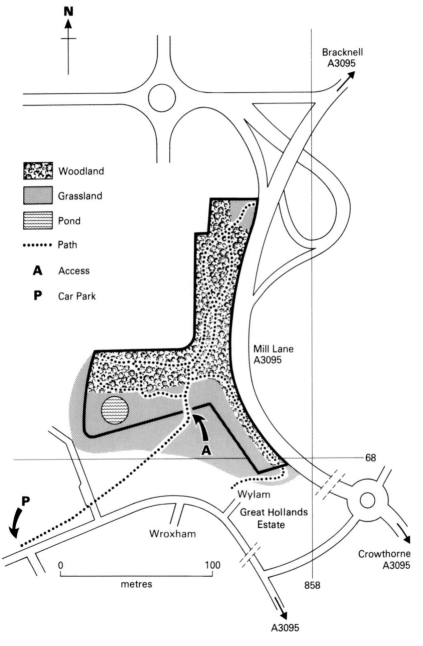

145

Oakley Hill

OS sheet 165; SU 753994

Nearest towns Chinnor, Thame and Princes Risborough

A 10 hectare (25 acre) area of old chalk downland and beech woodland. Just under half was purchased by BBONT in 1983. The rest was donated by Richard and Maisie Fitter in 1993.

Location

From Thame travel south-eastwards along the B4445 straight through Chinnor to the Upper Icknield Way at SP 760002. Park on the Icknield Way but do not drive along it. Walk south-westwards for 1 mile and turn left round the end of the quarry workings and walk uphill for 150 metres. The reserve is ahead of you.

Access

Open to the public. There may be sheep grazing, so no dogs please.

Description

The reserve consists of old chalk downland, some of which is colonised by scrub, and beech woodland. There are still open areas with typical downland plants including common rock-rose (flowering 5–9), wild thyme (5–8), Chiltern gentian (8–9), clustered bellflower (7–8), harebell (7–9), common spotted-orchid (6–8), and yellow-wort (6–10). Many butterflies can be expected on the wing in the summer months.

There is beech woodland in the upper half of the reserve which has in the past held yellow bird's-nest (6–8), white helleborine (5–7) and narrow-leaved helleborine (5–6).

Management

The reserve has suffered neglect for many years, but some of the scrub has been removed and the area is grazed by the BBONT sheep flock.

Any member of the public can sponsor the BBONT flock. The money helps to pay for the sheep's purchase, management and care. Sheep need regular attention to prevent the diseases and parasites which can afflict them. The flock is moved around the nature reserves as and when needed. Their grazing keeps down tough tall grasses and allows the smaller wild flowers to flourish.

The 150 strong flock of speckle-faced Beulahs, a mid-Wales breed, is supervised by a full-time BBONT Grasslands Officer helped by volunteers. Careful planning is needed to manage their grazing patterns to the benefit of the wild flowers, butterflies and other insects of the grassland reserves.

Each year BBONT has to decide which reserves are to be allowed to rest ungrazed and come into full flower. After the flowering and seeding time, the sheep return – welcomed by reserve managers, for by then the grass has grown tall.

Oakley Hill

OS sheet 165; SU 753994

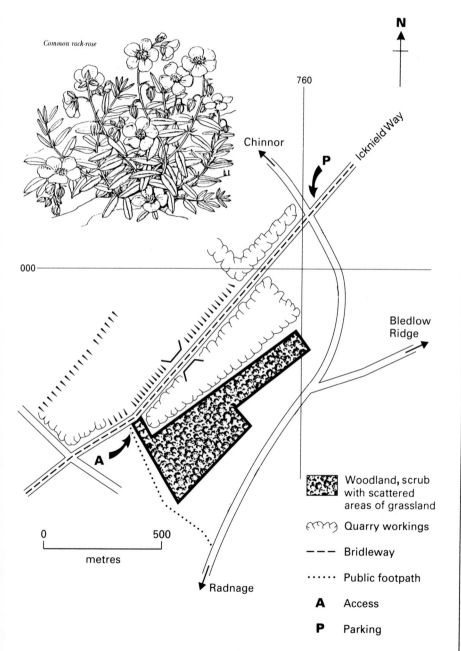

Common rock-rose

N

760

Chinnor

P

Icknield Way

000

Bledlow
Ridge

A

Radnage

0   500

metres

Woodland, scrub
with scattered
areas of grassland

Quarry workings

— — — Bridleway

· · · · · · Public footpath

A   Access

P   Parking

OPEN ACCESS NATURE RESERVES

147

Oxey Mead

OS sheet 164; SP 478107

Nearest town Oxford

Around 8 hectares (20 acres) of ancient meadow land. An SSSI, it was given to BBONT by the Inland Revenue who received it in lieu of death duties.

Location

The reserve lies close to the edge of Oxford. Leave Oxford on the A40 for Witney. It passes below the A43 Oxford by-pass and after about 1½ miles you reach a lay-by on the left. Park here and go over the stile following the public footpath to the east to reach the reserve. The River Thames forms the southern boundary.

Access

Open to the public but please keep to the footpath.

Description

Oxey (once Ox Hay) Mead is part of a larger area known as Yarnton Meadows. When the A40 was built in the 1930s, the land to its north was sold and ploughed. Oxey Mead has never been ploughed and has survived as an echo of a bygone age, being traditionally managed (by mowing for hay followed by grazing of the regrowth) before and after coming into BBONT's care.

The history of Yarnton Meadows dates back to before the Domesday Book when, as was usual, this village hay-land was held in common by the villagers. It was a lot meadow – each 'commoner' had rights to a strip of the meadow, and these strips were allocated in June when wooden balls carrying the commoner's names or marks were drawn from a bag. Once drawn, a swathe was cut from the strip and the new owner's initials cut into the ground with a knife. The luck of the draw gained the villager his lot for that year, and his harvest of its slightly better (or poorer) hay.

There is a close link between traditional management and richly diverse nature. In a flood meadow such as this there can be as many as 75 different species of plant, including perhaps 15 different wild grasses. Amongst the galaxy of wild flowers are great burnet (flowering 6–9), pepper-saxifrage (6–8) and devil's-bit scabious (6–10).

There is also an abundance of grasshoppers, spiders and beetles. Curlews, snipe and redshanks may perhaps be seen.

Management

Mowing at the end of June/beginning of July followed by cattle grazing until the end of November.

Additional note

Yarnton and Pixey Mead (alongside) are still owned jointly by local farmers with their rights in named cherrywood balls: Walter Jeffrey, Harry, Gilbert, Boat, Watery Molly, William of Bladon – not their own names, but those of the owners of the thirteenth century. Today's owners have not met recently to draw lots but they may take up the old tradition. Agreements have been made with English Nature to safeguard the wildlife of these meads.

Oxey Mead

OS sheet 164; SP 478107

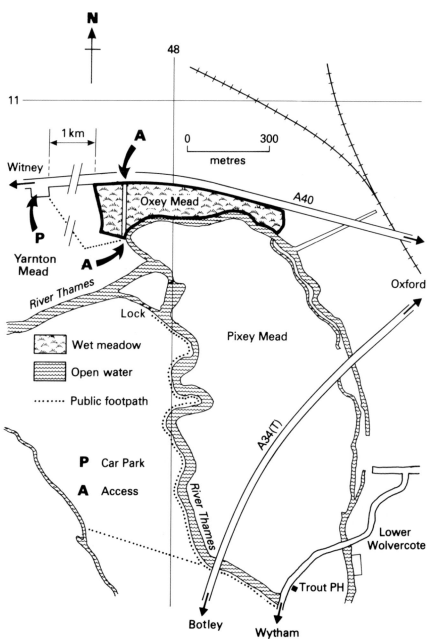

N

48

11

1 km

A

Witney

0   300

metres

Oxey Mead

A40

P

Yarnton
Mead

A

Oxford

River Thames

Lock

Pixey Mead

Wet meadow

Open water

Public footpath

A34(T)

P Car Park

A Access

River Thames

Lower
Wolvercote

Trout PH

Botley

Wytham

Pilch Field

OS sheets 152 & 165; SP 749321

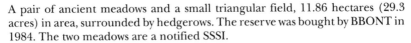

Nearest towns Buckingham and Winslow

A pair of ancient meadows and a small triangular field, 11.86 hectares (29.3 acres) in area, surrounded by hedgerows. The reserve was bought by BBONT in 1984. The two meadows are a notified SSSI.

Location
From Buckingham take the A421 towards Milton Keynes for about 3 miles and then take the unclassified road on the right, towards Great Horwood. Park on the verge near the sharp left-hand bend. The reserve is through the gate to the right of you and consists of the small triangular field plus the large field in front of it and a second large field to its right.

Access
Open to the public, but a local farmer has a grazing licence and no dogs are allowed when stock are grazing.

Description
The two ancient fields are marked with medieval ridge and furrow. Although they have been drained in part, they have escaped deep modern ploughing and there are still major soil differences which show themselves in the distribution of the wild flowers and wild grasses.

The drier areas have meadow barley, meadow oat-grass and quaking-grass. The quaking-grass is one of our most elegant wild grasses, its dainty panicles set dancing by the slightest breeze (hence its name) in June. Among the flowers seen are dwarf thistle (flowering 6–9), salad burnet (5–8), cowslip (4–5), dropwort (5–8), green-winged (5–6) and bee (6–7) orchids.

In spring, handsome marsh-marigold (kingcup) flowers (3–5) mark the damper soil. There are many wet 'flushes' fed by water seeping through the soil. Rushes, sedges and wetland wild flowers such as meadowsweet (6–9), marsh valerian (5–6) and the early marsh-orchid (5–7) grow readily here. One plant to watch out for is carnation sedge. Its leaves are pale bluish-green, rather like the colour of garden carnation leaves, hence its name.

There are plenty of butterflies, grasshoppers and other insects. Look out for the six-spot burnet moth, which can be seen flying on sunny days from June to August. It flies sluggishly and could be caught even on the wing by a nimble bird. However its gaudy black and red colouring is a warning to birds and other predators of its unpleasant taste.

Numerous birds use the bordering hedgerows – nesting warblers and resting kestrels are often seen. From time to time, green woodpeckers come to feed on the meadows. They have a particular liking for ants and Pilch Field has a number of yellow ant hills. These yellow ants tend to live on land which has not been disturbed by ploughing and are typical of ancient meadows.

Management
The fields are grazed by cattle.

Pilch Field

OS sheets 152 & 165; SP 749321

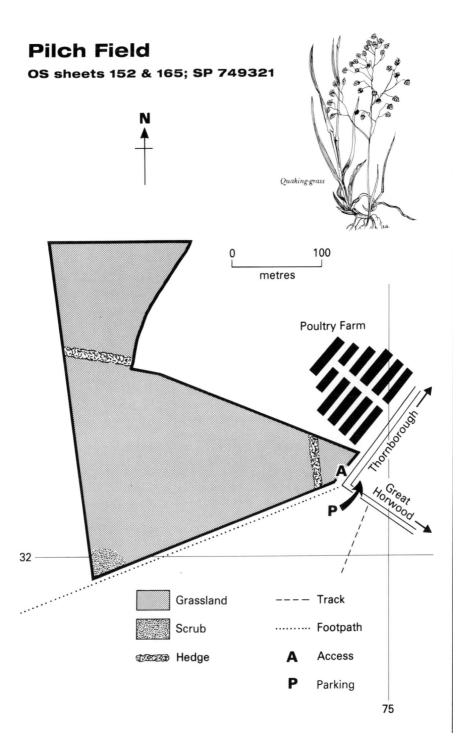

N

Quaking-grass

0   100
metres

Poultry Farm

Thornborough

Great Horwood

A

P

32

	Grassland		– – –	Track
	Scrub		··········	Footpath
	Hedge		**A**	Access
			P	Parking

75

Pitstone Hill

OS sheet 165; SP 955148

Nearest towns Aylesbury, Tring and Wendover

The reserve consists of 21.85 hectares (54 acres) of chalk grassland. It is an SSSI on licence from Buckinghamshire County Council. It is within the Chilterns Area of Outstanding Natural Beauty and makes a fine outing for the nearby views alone. A section of Grimm's Ditch runs through most of its length.

Location

From the roundabout situated on the A41 just west of Tring follow the unclassified road north-east past Tring to Tring Wharf. Take the B488 north-east to the T-junction at SP 950155. Turn right towards Aldbury. The car park is on your right on the brow of the hill.

Access

Open to the public. Dogs must be kept on a lead.

Description

Pitstone Hill has a steep scarp face, with chalk exposed for some of its length. The reserve faces southwards to Aldbury Nowers Wood. It is a very good piece of grazed chalk grassland, and although the gentler slopes at the top have had artificial fertilizers applied, the turf of the steeper slopes has escaped this treatment. (Artificial fertilization encourages the coarser grasses which then grow to overwhelm the slighter wild flowers.)

For the botanist, the steep slopes carry most of the classic chalkland flowers. A prime example is the pasqueflower, its flowering (4–6) often coinciding with Easter, presumably the origin of its name ('pasque' comes from the French for 'passion').

The butterflies here are just as interesting as the flowers they depend upon. Female butterflies lay their eggs on the plants upon which their caterpillars will feed. Often, the caterpillars need a specific foodplant, and consequently the butterflies are only found where this plant grows. For instance, on this reserve such localised butterflies include the chalkhill blue, which lays its eggs on the horseshoe vetch (flowering 5–7), the small blue, which needs kidney vetch (4–9), and the brown argus, which chooses the common rock-rose (5–9).

There are numerous ant hills made by the yellow ant. Of a considerable age, they are worth protecting on any nature reserve where they occur. The worker ants are rarely seen, since they forage mainly below ground. From time to time in summer, however, perhaps in response to such things as air temperature and static electricity (a sign of dry air), winged males and females swarm out in a nuptial flight, after which the males die and the females live on to become egg-laying 'queens'.

Skylarks, meadow pipits and other birds sing here, on this truly delightful site.

Management

The reserve is grazed by sheep. Scrub has been removed during the past few years and needs to be kept under control.

Pitstone Hill

OS sheet 165; SP 955148

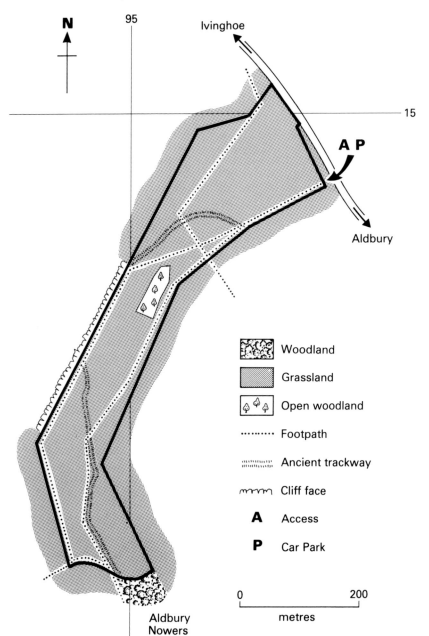

Woodland

Grassland

Open woodland

Footpath

Ancient trackway

Cliff face

A Access

P Car Park

0   200

metres

Seven Barrows

OS sheet 174; SU 329827

Nearest towns Wantage and Lambourn

5.3 hectares (13 acres) of ungrazed chalk grassland encompassing a number of prehistoric burial mounds. It is a site of national importance, both for its archaeological interest and as a nature reserve. It is an SSSI and is managed by BBONT in agreement with the owner.

Location

Start from Lambourn, to the south-west of Wantage. Leave Lambourn northwards on the B4001 for 1½ miles to Mile End and then fork left for a mile. As the map shows, the reserve lies along the north side of the road, between it and a bridleway. Cars should be parked in the marked car park. Please do not drive across the grass.

Access

Open to the public.

Description

This is an ancient and atmospheric site. There are in fact over 30 burial mounds of various kinds in and around the reserve, mostly dating from the Bronze Age. The mounds have made it physically difficult to use the land for anything but grazing. It has never been ploughed.

The reserve is a precious fragment of the flower-rich grassland which until comparatively recently was widespread over the chalk of the Berkshire Downs. Over 150 different plant species have been recorded, including the horseshoe vetch (flowering 5–7), and common rock-rose (5–9), the delicate blue harebell (7–9) nodding in the breeze, and the sturdier, purple-blue clustered bellflower (5–9).

Old chalk grassland also carries a notable butterfly population. A large number of species have been recorded here, including several which are rapidly declining along with the remaining areas of untouched chalk grassland which are not protected as nature reserves. The key here is the plant on which the butterfly lays its eggs. The chalkhill blue, for example, will only lay eggs on horseshoe vetch, and is not seen when this plant is absent. The small blue and the brown argus choose kidney vetch and common rock-rose respectively. The fast flying dark green fritillary is worth looking out for in July. It is often seen, although the hairy violet, the plant it normally lays its eggs near, has not so far been recorded here.

Management

The invading scrub is being removed and the flat turf is mown twice yearly in spring and late summer. Volunteers mow the 'disc and bowl' barrows when necessary, and the site is grazed by sheep for part of the year.

Seven Barrows

OS sheet 174; SU 329827

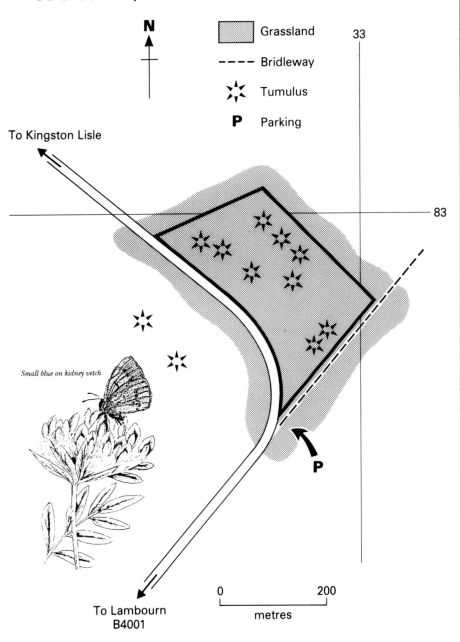

N

▨	Grassland
- - -	Bridleway
☆	Tumulus
P	Parking

33

83

To Kingston Lisle

Small blue on kidney vetch

P

0   200
metres

To Lambourn
B4001

The Slade, Bloxham

OS sheet 151; SP 423354

Nearest towns Bloxham and Banbury

A mixed reserve including a stretch of disused railway, wet meadow and woodland. It covers 2.2 hectares (5½ acres) and is leased to BBONT by Oxfordshire County Council.

Location

From Banbury take the A361 towards Chipping Norton; go through Bloxham and on the southern edge of the town park on the verge by the playing fields on the right. From the gate take the footpath which follows the northern boundary of the playing field to a stile in the north-west corner. Continue through the next field along the northern boundary fence to the stile just past the last house. This leads into the reserve.

Access

Open to the public. The wet meadow and woodland are rather delicate habitats, so please keep to the pathway.

Description

The reserve has a good variety of habitats within a small area. There is a disused railway line, wet meadow and woodland. Two small streams meet in the middle and flow out at the north-east corner of the reserve. Over 170 different plants have been recorded and the site is also good for bird life and butterflies, although no very rare or restricted species have been recorded here.

One feature of interest is a small mound, the ruin of a 'pest house' serving Bloxham. A pest house was once a fairly common village feature – a cottage where those with contagious diseases could be isolated. Here it was surrounded by a small moat which healthy villagers dared not cross – request for food and news were shouted across. Food was left on a special stone by the moat, to be taken in when the villagers had retreated.

This pest house was apparently in use into the early years of this century. In the smallpox epidemic of 1850, of all the 'patients' only one man came out alive.

Management

Work has included cutting areas of the wet meadow, maintenance of footpaths, fences and stiles and the creation of ponds. Woodland management includes coppicing and also pollarding willows.

The reserve is used by a local Wildlife WATCH group who hold regular monthly meetings at the site to compile their nature diary. The group has collected a great deal of information and has gained a good understanding of how the reserve changes with the seasons. The young people are also involved with the management work on the reserve, assisting with a variety of tasks.

This is a good example of how reserves can be used to encourage involvement in nature conservation. Several BBONT nature reserves are used regularly by Wildlife WATCH groups in this way.

The Slade, Bloxham

OS sheet 151; SP 423354

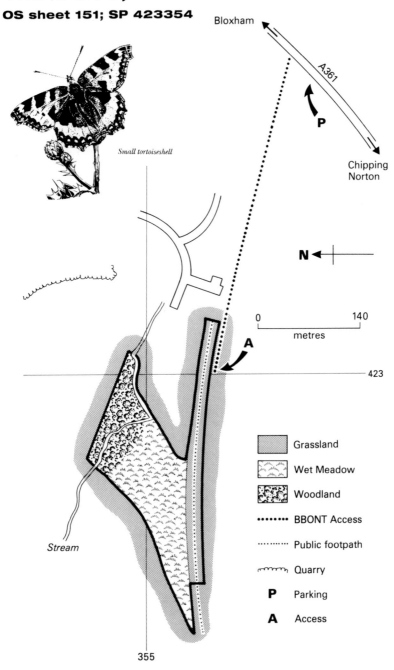

Small tortoiseshell

Bloxham

A361

P

Chipping
Norton

N

0   140
metres

A

423

Stream

355

Grassland

Wet Meadow

Woodland

•••••••• BBONT Access

·········· Public footpath

Quarry

P   Parking

A   Access

Sole Common Pond

OS sheet 174; SU 413707

Nearest town Newbury

A pond with nearby areas of bog and heath and woodland, 4 hectares (10 acres) in extent, managed since 1975 by agreement with the owners.

Location

Leave Newbury westwards on the A4. Quite soon, at the edge of Speen, fork right along the B4000 to Wickham and Lambourn. After 2½ miles, turn right into the Boxford road and 350 metres further on you come to a track on the left. Park at the side of the road. The reserve lies in the valley alongside the track as the map opposite shows. The reserve is unfenced, the boundaries following the lip of the valley.

Access

Open to the public. Please avoid walking around the edges of the pond and along the floor of the valley on the sphagnum bog, as these areas are easily damaged. Dogs are not permitted on the reserve.

Description

Here we have one of the few remaining bogs in our three counties. The valley is fed by a small stream running from the sandy soil and provides just the right conditions of nutrient-poor, acidic, waterlogging for a bog to develop. The bog has been damaged by over-collection of bog moss in the past, but is recovering under BBONT's management.

In the bog, round-leaved sundew can be seen (flowering 6–8), growing on its surface. Look also for bogbean (5–7), marsh St John's-wort (6–9) and the polypody fern.

The small pond is well worth studying, being rich in wildlife within its border of mosses. The inhabitants and visitors change with the seasons. In the summer months dragonflies are particularly abundant.

Other habitats in the reserve include heathland on the northern slopes (being invaded by birch and bracken), and mature woodland with oak, birch, beech, sweet chestnut and some conifers on the southern slopes.

Of the bird life, woodcock are perhaps most interesting for they are not common within BBONT's boundaries. They are waders which have deserted the open marshes to live in woodland. However they need wettish woods. Their long and rather sensitive beaks can only probe soft ground for worms and other food. When disturbed they twist away amongst the trees. Wood warblers are also here in spring and summer. They perch in the woodland canopy, their notes accelerating and blurring into a shimmering trill every ten seconds or so. They like woods with a rather open floor, such as this.

Management

Recent management has cleared birch from large areas of the bog and heath. A weir has been constructed to maintain the water as a constant level. Future plans include controlling the remaining birch and reducing the bracken on the heath.

158

Sole Common Pond

OS sheet 174; SU 413707

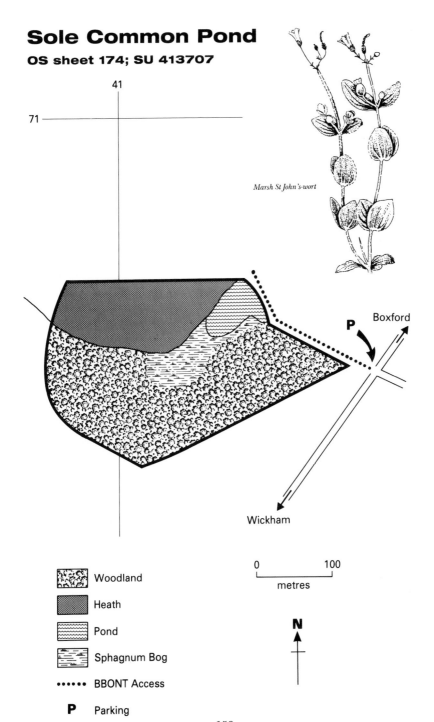

Marsh St John's-wort

Boxford

P

Wickham

Woodland

Heath

Pond

Sphagnum Bog

•••••• BBONT Access

P Parking

0   100
metres

N

Vicarage Pit

OS sheet 164; SP 403056

Nearest town Witney

A water-filled pit subleased from Oxfordshire County Council who declared it a Local Nature Reserve in 1976. The reserve totals 9.2 hectares (23 acres).

Location

The reserve lies south-east of Witney on the north side of the minor road which runs between Hardwick and Stanton Harcourt and is about 1 mile west of the last village. The car park is inside the gates at the south-east corner of the reserve.

Access

Open to the public, but please note that if interesting wildfowl are seen from the hide, it is best to remain there if you want to watch them. If you move from the hide, these birds tend to leave, and fly to the neighbouring pits to the south. They are also disturbed when anglers are present (see under Management below).

Description

This water-filled pit has steep banks and deep water on its north, west and south sides while its eastern end gradually becomes shallow and ideal for the presently expanding reedbed. In the existing willow 'carr' a small colony of common spotted-orchid (flowering 6–8) can be found.

The main attraction of the reserve, however, is the chance to see a range of interesting wildfowl which use the pit for both feeding and refuge. This is particularly so in the winter when pochard, coot and mallard arrive along with black-headed gull and mute swan.

In the summer breeding birds include great crested grebe in the reed fringe while common tern are now breeding on the tern rafts in the middle of the pit. With the expanding reedbed and management of the 'carr', species such as reed and sedge warbler are now benefiting from this important habitat.

Management

Young willows have been removed from the gravel areas in the north-east corner in order to create a suitable nesting ground for the little ringed plover, which did nest here in the past (attracted by wide expanses of bare ground, especially shingle, alongside open water). Further clearance of willows has allowed the expansion of reed and sedge beds. The grassy areas are mown in autumn, after the summer flowers have set seed. There is a hide on the south side of the pit.

The lake has been stocked with a variety of fish by the angling club which has private fishing rights, leased directly from the owner.

Vicarage Pit
OS sheet 164; SP 403056

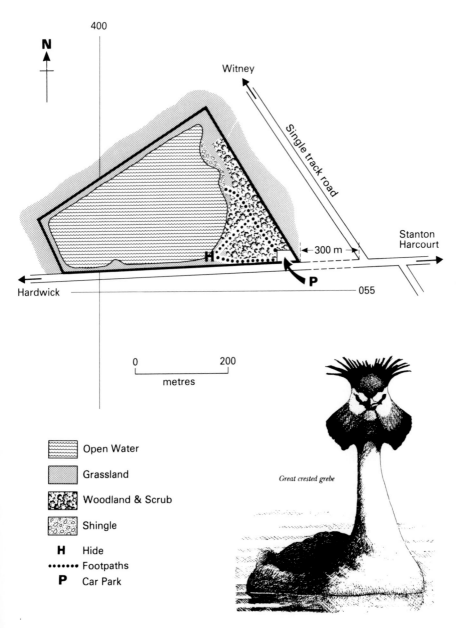

400

N

Witney

Single track road

Stanton Harcourt

← 300 m →

H

P

Hardwick

055

0   200

metres

Open Water

Grassland

Woodland & Scrub

Shingle

H Hide

•••••• Footpaths

P Car Park

Great crested grebe

Warren Bank

OS sheet 175; SU 653859

Nearest town Wallingford

An area of chalk grassland and scrub, 2.8 hectares (7 acres) in area. It has been managed by BBONT in agreement with the owners since 1972.

Location

Leave Wallingford to the east, cross the river and after ¼ mile turn right along the A4074 towards Reading. After 2 miles turn left at the White House Inn. Turn left at the crossroads and right after 100 metres through the hamlet of Hailey and on up a rough track. Enter the woods and after 100 metres park on the right. Follow the track to the right leading to the field gate. Walk straight ahead for 100 metres keeping to the right of the wire dividing fence. A stile and notice board on the left mark the entrance to the reserve.

Access

Open to the public. The small plantation near the bottom of the slope is not part of the reserve, and the owners shoot there from time to time. Please delay your visit if a shoot is in progress.

Description

Here, surrounded by scrub, is a small relic of the chalk grasslands that once covered most of the downs. The grassland is divided into three paddocks in which downland plants such as marjoram (flowering 7–9), cowslip (4–5) and bee orchid (6–7) can be seen. Plants typical of chalk downland include field scabious (7–9) and chalk milkwort, with flowers (5–6) of a piercing gentian-blue. Look out for these here and at other grassland reserves.

The history of downland fragments such as this is interesting from a conservation point of view. When covered with flowers, these fragments can be as colourful as the stained glass in a village church, but are in fact much older.

Towards the end of the Ice Age, trees invaded Britain (around 8,000 years ago) creating a tangled wildwood in all but the wettest and bleakest places. Neolithic (new Stone Age) tribes, the first farmers, crossed into England bringing cattle, sheep, goats and pigs. They chose the lightly wooded soils of the gravel islands in the river valleys and the chalk downland for their settlements. They felled and fired the trees to produce clearings for harvests of corn while their animals grazed (and in time destroyed) the surrounding woodland. The downs gradually became open.

Soil impoverishment and continual grazing meant that it became difficult for trees to recolonize the downland. Grazing and poor manuring (mainly by sheep), century after century encouraged small plants at the expense of large ones. These made up for their lack of size in the brilliance of their flowers.

Ploughing in recent decades has destroyed many of these grasslands so the remaining fragments need all the protection they can get.

Management

Some scrub has been removed but more needs to be taken out. The grassland is grazed by sheep.

Warren Bank

OS sheet 175; SU 653859

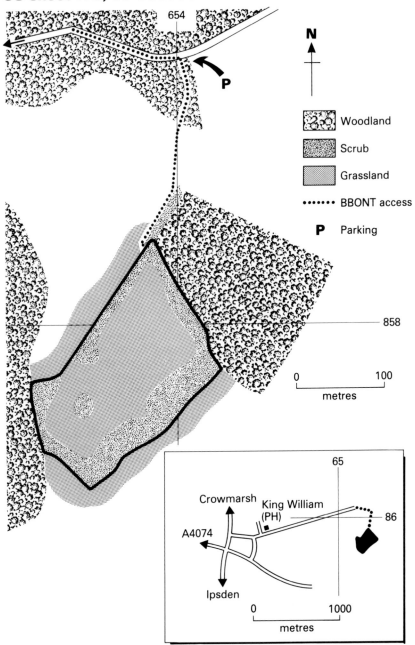

654

N

P

Woodland

Scrub

Grassland

•••••• BBONT access

P Parking

858

0   100

metres

65

Crowmarsh King William
(PH)

86

A4074

Ipsden

0   1000

metres

Watts Reserve (White Shute)
OS sheet 174; SU 331772

Nearest town Lambourn

Watts Reserve consists of the eastern part of the White Shute SSSI. The SSSI gained its name from the adjacent track called the White Shute By-way. This 1.4 hectare (3.5 acre) chalk grassland site was purchased by BBONT in 1991 as a result of a monetary bequest from the late Miss Lilian Maud Watts.

Location

At the centre of Lambourn, go from Lambourn Church along Newbury Street and turn right into Station Road. Turn right again into Edward's Hill and then left into Greenway. Follow the Greenway to Lambourn School and park nearby. Go down the track from the school for about a mile. The Watts Reserve will then be on the left.

Access

Open to the public. Please keep dogs under control when sheep are grazing.

Description

As the reserve lies on a steep south-west facing slope it is a natural sun trap and is often warm and sunny in spring and summer. This, coupled with the diverse nature of long undisturbed chalk grassland, has resulted in the site containing over 90 species of wild flowers, of which some are nationally rare. There are also over 16 species of grasses. The most common grass is upright brome. This is interspersed with quaking-grass, sheep's fescue, downy oat-grass and crested hair-grass, to name but a few.

Displays of common spotted-orchid (flowering 6–8), southern marsh-orchid (6–8) and fragrant (6–7) orchid make the reserve well worth a summer visit. In addition to these, wild flowers such as clustered bellflower (6–10), lady's bedstraw (6–9), rough hawkbit (6–10) and autumn gentian (8–10) have encouraged over 32 species of butterfly to the reserve. These include the chalkhill blue, green hairstreak, dingy skipper and brown argus. Special note should be made of firstly the uncommon Duke of Burgundy butterfly which relies on the cowslip (4–5) to complete its life cycle, and secondly the rare marsh fritillary butterfly which uses the devil's-bit scabious (6–10) as a foodplant for its caterpillars.

The reserve also contains small areas of scrub in addition to the grassland. This is made up of hazel, blackthorn and bramble, and is found in the very centre of the reserve or along its margins. The scrub provides a good contrast to the open grassland, with much needed cover for many small birds.

Management

A stockproof fence was built around the reserve in 1991 by BBONT. This allows sheep to graze the reserve and so maintain the vulnerable chalk grassland. This is done in two ways, firstly by stopping further invasion of scrub onto the open grassland and secondly by preventing the coarse grasses from overshadowing the more fragile wild flowers. The fence also prevents motorcyclists riding across the reserve and damaging the grassland, as has happened before. It is hoped in future to take detailed species surveys of the site.

Watts Reserve (White Shute)

OS sheet 174; SU 331772

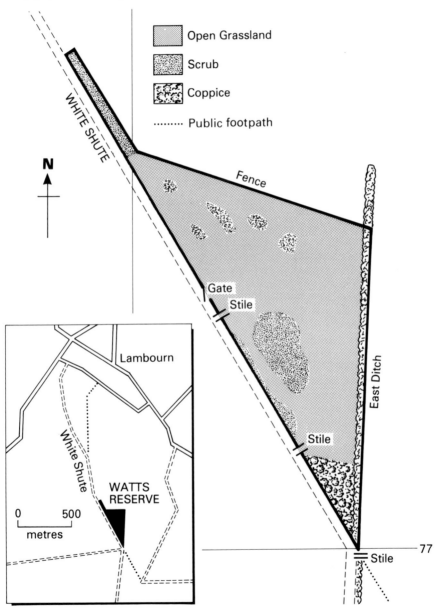

Open Grassland

Scrub

Coppice

.... Public footpath

WHITE SHUTE

N

Fence

Gate
Stile

Lambourn

White Shute

WATTS RESERVE

0   500
metres

East Ditch

Stile

Stile

77

Weston Turville Reservoir
OS sheet 165; SP 859095

Nearest towns Aylesbury and Wendover

An old reservoir with 4.8 hectares (12 acres) of surrounding land, this is an SSSI managed by BBONT by agreement with the British Waterways Board since 1966.

Location

From Wendover take the A413 north; turn right after one mile opposite the Marquis of Granby public house. Park in the lay-by after 500 metres, and the reserve is on your right.

Access

Open to the public along the perimeter path only.

Description

The open water is leased by the British Waterways Authority to the local sailing and angling clubs. BBONT's agreement covers only the surrounding land and reedbeds. However BBONT, since 1963, has had shooting rights over the whole area. These rights are not exercised.

The reservoir was constructed in 1795 to supply water to an arm of the Grand Union Canal. Over the years a good many wetland plants have colonised its margins. There is now an extensive reedbed, and a marshy fen. In addition to the reed (its tassels notable in later summer), plants include the lesser bulrush and early marsh-orchid (flowering 5–7). Orange balsam (6–8), less familiar than the purplish flowered Himalayan (or Indian) balsam, is also present. Both balsams are non-native species.

There are good breeding colonies of reed warbler. This bird is perhaps less likely to be seen than heard: its song is a flow of 'churr-churr-churr ... chirruc-chirruc-chirruc ...' notes. It makes a beautifully woven cup nest, slung between the reed stems, deep enough to prevent eggs or chicks being tossed out when the reeds sway in the wind. The site might attract cuckoos in spring as the reed warbler is one of the cuckoo's main hosts. The reserve is also the only regular Buckinghamshire breeding site of the water rail. This bird too, is much more often heard than seen, its call sounding like a piglet squealing. It can regularly be heard all year round.

The reserve is renowned as an autumn roost area for swallows which gather into large flocks before leaving (suddenly, when wind and weather are right) on migration. Starlings also roost here in some numbers in autumn.

The reserve is a good place to observe winter wildfowl, both overwintering and on passage to and from breeding grounds to the north of Britain. In April 1988, for example, two female eider ducks were seen here – the first record of this species in Buckinghamshire.

Management

Attempts have been made to remove sycamore from the wetland area, and the marsh area is kept free of sallow scrub.

Weston Turville Reservoir

OS sheet 165; SP 859095

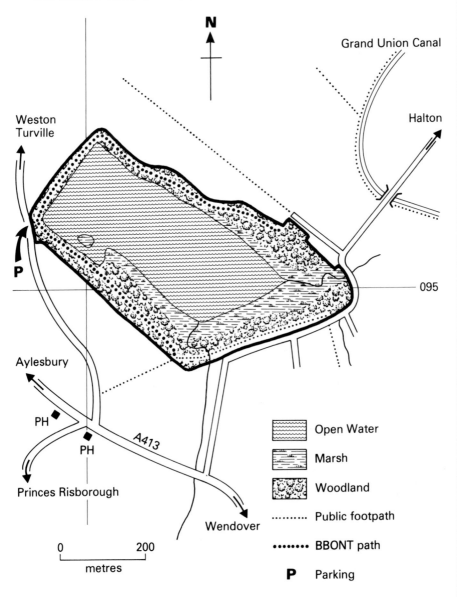

Open Water

Marsh

Woodland

.... Public footpath

•••••••• BBONT path

P Parking

Westwell Gorse
OS sheet 163; SP 221113

Nearest towns Burford and Witney

A small area of grassland and scrub, 2.28 hectares (5.7 acres) in area. It is leased from the owners.

Location

Leave Burford westwards on the A40 for 1 mile, and turn left along the B4425. After one mile park on the verge beyond the farm track on the right. The reserve is on the right at this point.

The road boundary of the reserve is marked by a Cotswold dry stone wall, which has been restored by the British Trust for Conservation Volunteers (BTCV) over a number of years.

Access

Open to the public.

Description

The reserve is on the Oxfordshire-Gloucestershire border, and is set in the north-western corner of Westwell Parish. The 1770 Enclosure Award set aside this area for raising furze (gorse) and other fuel for the benefit of the poor of Westwell Parish. It was originally divided into seven sections, one being cut each year for fuel. Although this practice came to an end in the middle of last century, the land was administered by the Westwell Charities until 1993.

BBONT was interested in the site as an example of unimproved grassland among the surrounding intensively farmed arable fields. The underlying rock is limestone, making the soil alkaline. A variety of wild flowers can be seen, including pyramidal orchid (6–8), common twayblade (6–7), fragrant orchid (6–7), dropwort (5–8), harebell (7–9), field scabious (7–9), purple milk-vetch (5–7) and the downy-fruited sedge (5–7), which is a nationally rare plant. More than 200 different plant species have now been recorded on this reserve.

There is a variety of butterflies and other insects. The scrub area is also attractive to nesting and roosting birds.

Management

There was no maintenance prior to BBONT's lease, and as a result scrub had invaded the grassland. Scrub has been and is being removed. The grassland is cut late every autumn and the grass cuttings raked off, allowing delicate plants to flourish, as well as encouraging the downy-fruited sedge to dramatically increase in numbers. New species, not seen here for many years, are now being recorded.

Rides cut through the scrub allow the visitor to wander through these parts of the reserve. The extensive lichen growths on the blackthorn are worth inspecting. The rides also provide sheltered open areas for butterflies.

Dutch elm disease in the 1970s destroyed the elm woodland which once covered about a third of the site on the western side. Elm regrowth is being encouraged (it can produce suckers from its root system) and new trees have been planted in the woodland area.

Westwell Gorse

OS sheet 163; SP 221113

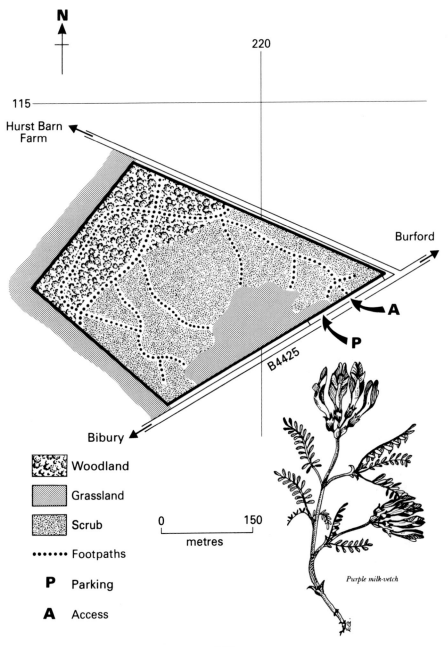

N

220

115

Hurst Barn Farm

Burford

A

P

B4425

Bibury

Woodland

Grassland

Scrub

•••••• Footpaths

P Parking

A Access

0   150
metres

Purple milk-vetch

Whitecross Green Wood

OS sheet 164; SP 600150

Nearest towns Oxford and Bicester

A 62 hectare (156 acres) woodland. It is an SSSI bought by BBONT in 1984.

Location
Leave Oxford northwards along the A34. Take the unclassified road to the right to Islip. Turn left in Islip towards Merton and take the first right through Oddington, Charlton-on-Otmoor and Murcott. One mile past Murcott there is a small cottage on the left, immediately opposite the reserve. Go through the wooden gate opposite. The car park is through the second gate. Please shut both gates as domestic animals graze along the track.

Access
Open to the public along all rides. Dogs are not permitted on the reserve.

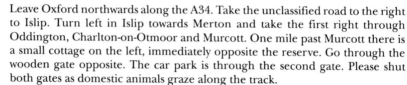

Description
The reserve straddles the Oxfordshire/Buckinghamshire county boundary. The small section in Buckinghamshire formed part of the Royal Forest of Bernwood. The wood was shown on a map of 1590, and a large boundary bank and ditch can still be seen. It is an ancient woodland and, as to be expected, harbours a great number of plants – the total recorded at present stands at 200 different species.

Unfortunately, between 1963 and 1965, over half this old wood was felled and replanted with conifers by the Forestry Commission. However, the rides through the pines are still rich in wild flowers and busy with insects of all kinds. The remainder of the wood consists mainly of blackthorn/hawthorn thickets and overgrown hazel coppice with some oak and ash standards. Among the wild flowers to be seen here are bluebells (flowering 4–6), ramsons (4–6), yellow archangel (5–6) and enchanter's nightshade (6–8). After removal of the pines, the reserve will gradually be restored to native woodland. This will be a slow process, taking 50 years or more, but future generations will benefit from our efforts. Ecologists are already interested in studying the effects of BBONT's management on wildlife within the wood.

Mammals seen include fallow and muntjac deer. The many butterflies include black hairstreak, purple emperor, wood white and marbled white. Nightingales, and grasshopper warblers nest here.

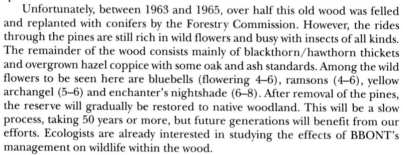

Management
The Scots pines will be thinned and eventually removed to provide a cash crop. The pine area will be returned to native high forest. Part of the neglected hazel is being coppiced to allow light to reach the woodland soil and encourage the growth of wild flowers associated with coppice woodlands. The rides are managed by mowing to control the growth of scrub and coarse grasses which would crowd out the less vigorous wild flowers.

BBONT has created further open areas along the central ride. Some have been recolonized by shrubs and trees while others are kept as grassland by mowing. The ponds are being cleared of silt and surrounding scrub.

Whitecross Green Wood

OS sheet 164; SP 600150

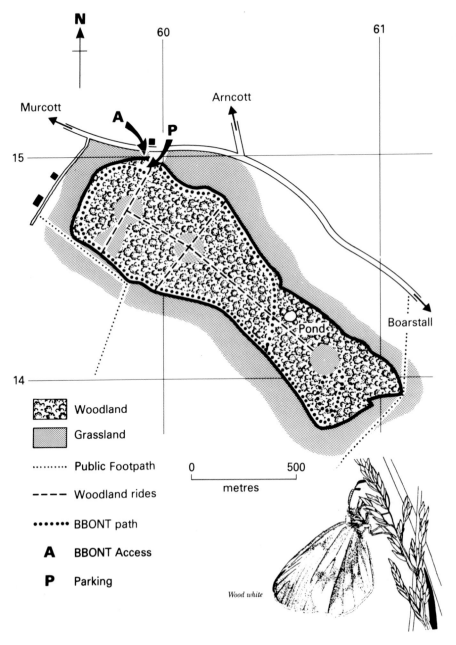

Wood white

Legend:

- Woodland
- Grassland
- .... Public Footpath
- – – – Woodland rides
- •••••• BBONT path
- **A** BBONT Access
- **P** Parking

0   500
metres

Murcott
Arncott
Boarstall
Pond

Wildridings Copse

OS sheet 175; SU 857688

Nearest town Bracknell

An area of ancient, semi-natural woodland, 1.2 hectares (3 acres) in area. It is situated on the Southern Industrial Estate in Bracknell, next to the headquarters of Panasonic UK who lease the site to BBONT. Panasonic funded the initial management of the reserve and have provided an endowment for its future.

Location
Take the A329 from Reading. Leave at the Bracknell roundabout. Take the second exit signposted for the Southern Industrial Centre. At the next roundabout turn left and continue until just after a zebra crossing. Here turn right into Doncaster Road and then left into Willoughby Road, opposite the ICC building. Wildridings Copse is on the left.

Access
Please keep to the footpath. The fence between the reserve and the Panasonic building is alarmed.

Description
Wildridings Copse is a remnant of a much larger ancient semi-natural wood. It is over 200 years old and is present on the Roques map of 1761. The copse contains 20 plants which are indicators of ancient woodland and so is likely to be much older than this.

As ancient woodland supports far more wildlife than planted, or reafforested woodland, it is a diverse nature reserve within a relatively built-up urban area. It is possible to find 22 species of tree here, including holly, English elm, aspen and eared willow, the latter being regionally scarce.

The wandering path that runs from the north to the south of the reserve and crosses an equally meandering seasonal stream, is an ideal route to view this diversity. Hazel coppice is found throughout this mixed deciduous woodland which has lead to a rich ground cover of flowering plants including bluebells (4–6), foxgloves (6–9) and honeysuckle (6–10).

The eastern side of the reserve contains many oak trees, and a row of mature 'crack' willows dividing the area in two. In the north-western corner, hazel trees (rather than the many stemmed hazel coppice) provide a contrast to an upper canopy of mainly ash coppice and birch. On the western side, fruit-bearing trees, such as crab apple and thorn, are found scattered among the other trees. This is the most diverse area with plants such as herb-Robert (4–11) and bugle (4–6) which occur in no other part of the wood.

The various trees provide cover for 21 species of bird, including the great spotted woodpecker, blackcap and bullfinch. Other animals also benefit from the reserve, and the orange-tip is one of many butterflies found here.

Management
Footpaths and bridges have been constructed. A hedge and trees have been planted. The new hedge needs maintaining, the paths and ditches need annual clearance. The planting and coppicing of the wood is an ongoing process.

Wildridings Copse

OS sheet 175; SU 857688

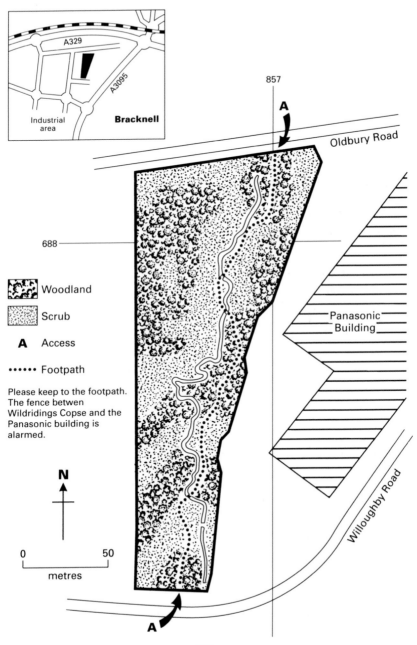

Woodland

Scrub

A Access

•••••• Footpath

Please keep to the footpath.
The fence betwen
Wildridings Copse and the
Panasonic building is
alarmed.

N

0   50
metres

Woodsides Meadow, Wendlebury

OS sheet 164; SP 556177

Nearest towns Oxford and Bicester

An old hayfield of 3.5 hectares (9 acres). Part of a larger SSSI, it was purchased by BBONT in 1989.

Location

From the A34 between Oxford and Bicester, take the B4027 south to Islip. In Islip take the road for Merton. You pass roads for Oddington, and then after about 3 miles the road for Charlton-on-Otmoor joins on the right. Opposite is a farm road running past Home Farm. This farm road is badly pitted and must be endured for about ¾ mile. Park at the end, just before the railway. Parking is limited so please take care not to obstruct the passage of other vehicles.

The route to the reserve lies to the right, along the green lane. Follow this to the end where it turns sharply left. You will be faced by a pair of gates on either side of the railway, which should be locked. Pay attention to the warning signs – the railway is in use and trains must be expected from time to time. Past the gate on the far side of the railway lies a track leading to the right, to the field which comprises the reserve.

Access

Open to the public.

Description

The reserve is one of a series of exceptionally rich wild flower meadows, which are rather a rare feature of the countryside today. Its wildlife value was not discovered until the 1970s, but surveys have shown that there are over a hundred different species of grasses and wild flowers growing. With no disturbance to the ground, their distribution tends to map differences in dampness and other factors in the soil below.

An example of this is the three species of buttercup present here. The meadow buttercup is the most abundant (flowering 5–8). It has smooth unfurrowed flower stalks with bright yellow flowers. The creeping buttercup (5–9) is the one most often seen as a weed in damp gardens, with runners and furrowed flower stalks. It competes well on wettish heavy soil. Also seen here is the bulbous buttercup (the first to flower, 4–6) with a swelling at the base of the stem and green sepals which turn back below the flower. It prefers drier, limey soil.

There are also orchids here – the common spotted-orchid (6–7) and southern marsh-orchid (6–8). The ditches, frequently full of water, and hedges are other features.

Newts are found in a small pond near the entrance.

Management

Cutting for hay and grazing the 'aftermath' is traditional management. The hedges are progressively coppiced and laid. Fencing is replaced when appropriate.

Woodsides Meadow, Wendlebury

OS sheet 164; SP 556177

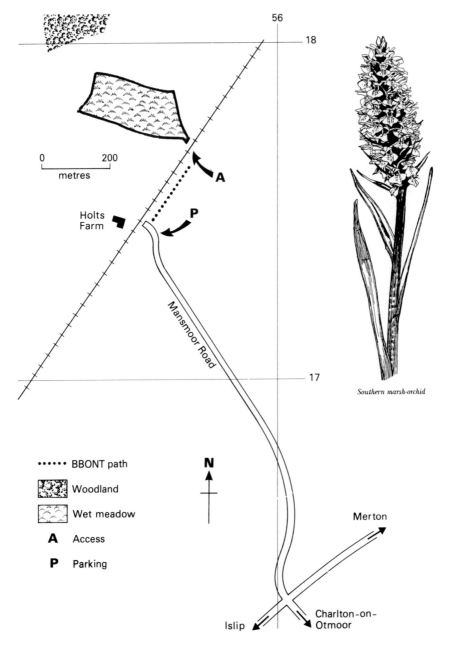

56

18

0   200
metres

Holts
Farm

A

P

Mansmoor Road

17

Southern marsh-orchid

••••• BBONT path

▨ Woodland

▨ Wet meadow

A Access

P Parking

N

Merton

Islip

Charlton-on-
Otmoor

Restricted access reserves

Details of these sites and permits to visit them are available from the nearest BBONT county office. Please send your request with an SAE at least four weeks before your visit. Please include the date you intend to visit the reserve.

Ardley Quarry
Oxfordshire

Calvert Jubilee and Extension
Buckinghamshire

Chawridge Bank
Berkshire

Crog Hill
Berkshire

Dancersend Waterworks
Buckinghamshire

Eversdown
Oxfordshire

Foxcote Reservoir
Buckinghamshire

Iffley Island
Oxfordshire

Lodge Wood
Berkshire

Munday Dean
Buckinghamshire

Oakley Parish Hedge
Buckinghamshire

Pitstone Fen
Buckinghamshire

Rack Marsh
Berkshire

Robertswood
Buckinghamshire

Swains Wood
Buckinghamshire

Windsor Hill
Buckinghamshire

Other wildlife sites of interest

Other wildlife sites in the three counties include:

Ambarrow Hill, Berks SU 825629. ½ mile south of Crowthorne Station. 4½ hectares of pine clad slopes belonging to the National Trust.

Aston Rowan National Nature Reserve, with Beacon Hill Forest Nature Reserve and Aston Hill, Oxon SU 7297. These areas of beechwood and chalk grassland lie astride the M40 between Stokenchurch and Lewknor.

Bagley Wood, Oxon SP 5102. Lying alongside the A34 on the south-west edge of Oxford, this wood is owned by St John's College. Parts of the original mixed woodland remain, but much is planted with conifers.

Banbury Sewage Farm, Oxon SP 474405. Five large meadows which are adjacent to the M40, but attract a large numbers of birds in winter and on migration.

Bernwood Forest, Bucks and Oxon SP 6009, 6110, 6210 and 6111. Bernwood Forest is the present-day name for the Forestry Commission woodlands lying north-east of Stanton St John. They include fragments of the ancient Royal Forest of Bernwood.

Black Park and Langley Park, Bucks TQ 0083. 4 miles north-east of Slough, Black Park is a country park with various woodlands and a lake, while Langley Park adjoining has some grassland, an arboretum and a farm.

Blenheim Park, Oxon SP 4316. On the edge of Woodstock, this contains fine old oaks, deer, insects and good waterfowl on the lake.

Bradenham Woods, Bucks. National Trust land. Bradenham Wood and Naphill Common lie between Bradenham and Naphill, SU 8397; Park Wood is ½ mile north of Bradenham SU 9298: a Grade 1 site for plateau and dip-slope beechwood with some oak on Naphill Common.

Bullingdon Bog (Lye Valley), Oxon SP 548058. Within Oxford's boundary and near the Churchill Hospital, at the junction of Girdlestone Road and The Slade. A relic valley fen area with good plants.

Bulmershe, Reading, Berks SU 752731. Lying beside Woodlands Avenue is a Pond with various surrounds, managed by the Reading Urban Wildlife Group.

Burghfield Common, Berks – see Wokefield Common.

Burnham Beeches and Dorneywood, Bucks SU 9585. ¾ mile west of Farnham Common lie these woodlands famous for their ancient pollard beech trees; they also contain oak and birch. Neighbouring East Burnham Common still has good heathland. Owned by City of London Corporation and the National Trust.

Buscot Park, Oxon SU 239973. Lying between Lechlade and Faringdon, this parkland includes a lake and heronry.

California Country Park, Berks SU 784652. Woodland, heath, bog and lake. Wokingham District Council.

Church Hill, West Wycombe, Bucks SU 828950. ¼ mile west of West Wycombe, a steep hill with chalk grassland, scrub and may old yew trees. National Trust.

Church Wood, Hedgerley, Bucks SU 975875. This is an outlier from Burnham Beeches, owned by the Royal Society for the Protection of Birds.

Cliveden, Bucks SU 913856. Lying 2½ miles north of Taplow, the well-known house and gardens are supplemented by some fine hanging beechwoods on the cliffs above the Thames. National Trust.

Cock Marsh, Berks SU 886868. 1 mile north of Cookham, 53 hectares of marshy meadows plus steep chalk slopes, owned by the National Trust.

Cookham Dean Common, Berks – see Maidenhead Thicket.

Cookham Moor, Berks SU 895853. In the middle of Cookham, 4 hectares of marshy grassland, owned by the National Trust.

Coombe Hill, Bucks SP 849066. Lying 1½ miles north of Wendover, 43 hectares of chalk grassland and scrub with some heathland on the clay-with-flints soil at the top – the summit at 269 metres is the highest point in the Chilterns. Owned by the National Trust.

Devil's Dip, Reading, Berks SU 690724. An old gravel pit managed by the Reading Urban Wildlife Group.

Dinton Pastures Country Park, Berks SU 785718. Flooded gravel pits. Wokingham District Council.

Edgbarrow Woods, Berks SU 837632. Heathland, pine woodland and bog, adjoining BBONT's OWLSMOOR BOG & HEATH reserve. Bracknell Forest Borough Council.

Englemere Pond Nature Trail, Berks SU 905685. Woodland, lake and heathland. Bracknell Forest Borough Council.

Finchampstead Ridges, Berks SU 808634, including Heath Pool and Simons Wood. ¾ mile west of Crowthorne Station, 43 hectares mainly of conifer woodland and heathland. National Trust.

Heath Pool, Berks – see Finchampstead Ridges.

Heron Island, Reading, Berks SU 702719. Once a thriving heronry before being damaged in the October 1987 storm. It is being replanted and managed by the Reading Urban Wildlife Group.

Hodgemoor Wood, Bucks SU 9693. 1 mile west of Chalfont St Giles, public footpaths run through extensive woodlands. Forestry Commission.

Hog and Hollowhill Woods, Bucks SU 823860. Near Medmenham, beech woodland – a Bucks CC countryside area with public access.

Hogback Wood, Bucks SU 927912. 1 mile west of Beaconsfield Station, 9 hectares of deciduous woodland owned by the National Trust.

Ivinghoe Beacon, Bucks SP 961169. 1½ miles north-east of Ivinghoe; together with Steps Hill and Clipper Down, good chalk grassland owned by the National Trust.

Langley Park, Bucks – see Black Park.

Lardon Chase and Lough Down, Berks SU 588809. ¼ mile north-west of Streatley, 27 hectares of downland owned by the National Trust.

Lodge Hill, Bucks SP 794001. 1½ miles south of Saunderton, astride the Ridgeway Path, an isolated hill with good chalk turf, wildflowers and butterflies.

Magdalen Meadow, Magdalen College in Oxford SP 524063. A fine fritillary meadow, with a herd of fallow deer in the adjoining park.

Maidenhead Thicket, Pinkney's Green and Cookham Dean Common, Berks SU 855810, 860825 and 863843. Situated to the west and north-west of Maidenhead, the National Trust here holds 248 hectares of land consisting of woodland, scrub and grasslands.

Moorend Common, Bucks SU 803905. 1 mile south-west of Lane End, a Chiltern common with good oakwood, scrub and grassland.

North Leigh Common, Oxon SP 402140. 1 mile north-east of North Leigh. 17 hectares of heathland, scrub and bog with a good variety of interesting flowers including western gorse.

Northmoor Hill Woods picnic site, Bucks SU 035891. Lying near Denham, this is an area of mixed woodland with alder carr.

Pangbourne Meadow, Bucks SU 640768. These 3 hectares of Thames-side meadow lie just below Pangbourne Bridge. National Trust.

Pixey Mead, Oxon – see Yarnton Mead.

Port Meadow, Oxon SP 4908. This fine Oxford grazing meadow lies 1½ miles north of Carfax.

Prestwood picnic site, Bucks SP 862020. A chalk downland setting for this Bucks County Council site.

Rushey Way Pond, Reading, Berks SU 752706. A large pond saved from development by the Reading Urban Wildlife Group.

Shepherds Meadow, Berks SU 850604. Wet meadows next to the River Blackwater. Bracknell Forest Borough Council.

Shotover Country Park, Oxon SU 5606. An Oxford City Council country park which includes a bracken-covered hillside with some oakwood.

Snelsmore Common, Berks SU 460710. 1½ miles north of Bewbury, this Newbury District Council park contains a fine stretch of heathland and bog.

Somerton Meads, Oxon SP 492302. ¾ mile north-west of Somerton, this is an important haunt for wildfowl.

Stockgrove Country Park with Rammamere Heath, Bucks SP 928300. A mixed woodland and lakes on acid sandy soil. Bucks County Council.

Stoke Common, Bucks SU 9885. 1 mile north-east of Stoke Poges, a stretch of overgrown heathland.

Stonesfield Common, Oxon SP 392165. ½ mile south of Stonesfield, some limestone grassland with many wildflowers.

Stonor Park, Oxon SU 740890. ¼ mile north-east of Stonor, an ancient deer park, notable also for its chalkland wildflowers. Owned by the Stonor family.

Stowe Park, Bucks SP 6636. 3 miles north-west of Buckingham, the school grounds include a 10 hectare woodland nature reserve.

Sutherland Grange, Berks SU 940772. Rough, unimproved neutral meadow. Royal Borough of Windsor and Maidenhead.

Sutton Courtenay Field Centre, Oxon SU 500920. A 6 hectare educational reserve 1½ miles south of Sutton Courtenay and in the grounds of Didcot Power Station.

Swyncombe Downs, Oxon SU 673912. 2½ miles east of Ewelme, this well-known viewpoint over the Thames valley has interesting wildflowers and some juniper.

Thatcham Reedbeds, Berks SU 500668. An area of reedbed, 2 miles west of Thatcham, important for birds and insects. Part is designated a Local Nature Reserve.

Virginia Water, Berks – see Windsor Great Park.

Watlington Hill and Park, Oxon SU 702935. 1 mile south-east of Watlington, the National Trust owns 60 hectares of beechwoods surrounding Watlington Park and 39 hectares of chalk grassland and scrub with many old yew trees.

Wendlebury Meads, Oxon SP 5617. National Nature Reserve 1½ miles north-west of Charlton-on-Otmoor. Lowland meadows with an exceptionally rich flora.

White Horse Hill, Oxon SU 300867. This historic site lies 2 miles south of Uffington. It comprises 95 hectares of National Trust land, chalk downland and farmland with outstanding wildflowers.

Widbrook Common, Berks SU 897840. 1 mile south of Cookham, 26 hectares of grazed marsh and grassland, owned by the National Trust.

Willen Lake, Bucks SP 8740. This first-class winter waterfowl resort is ¼ mile south of Willen in Milton Keynes.

Windsor Forest, Berks SU 9373. 2½ miles south of Windsor, this fragment of ancient oak forest is especially rich in beetles and other insects. It includes 18 hectares of High Standing Wood as a Forest Nature Reserve. Management is by the Crown Estates.

Windsor Great Park, Berks SU 97. Situated 1 mile south of Windsor this includes an extensive stretch of acid grassland, bracken and deciduous woodland, with some fine old oaks and three good waterfowl sites: Great Meadow Pond (965710), Obelisk Pond (977703) and Virginia Water (970690).

Wittenham Clumps, Oxon SU 570925. This well-known viewpoint lies 1 mile south-east of Little Wittenham, where the Nature Reserve is owned and managed by the Northmoor Trust.

Wokefield (or Burghfield) Common, Berks SU 635662. 1 mile north of Mortimer, this is a fine stretch of heathland with alder gullies and good fungi.

Wychwood Forest and Ponds, Oxon SP 3316. 1 mile north-east of Leafield, this remnant of once extensive ancient forest still has some fine patches of oakwood and limestone grassland.

Yarnton Mead, Oxon SP 4711. Lying south-west of Yarnton village, Pixey and Yarnton Meads are important stretches of old flower-rich meadowland managed in the same way for centuries – see the entry for BBONT's OXEY MEAD, page 154..

Gifts of reserves and grant aid for reserve purchases

We gratefully acknowledge the gifts of reserves from:

Mr & Mrs E. Hambly (Long Grove Wood)
Mr & Mrs J.A. Lamb (Lamb's Pool)
Miss Lilian Maud Watts (Watts Nature Reserve)
Mr & Mrs D. Porter (Blenheim Farm)
Mr & Mrs R. Fitter (extension to Oakley Hill)
Mrs Vera Paul OBE (extension to Warburg Reserve, warden's house and flat)

BBONT thanks the following for their generosity in helping us to purchase reserves:

Miss Diana Alderson
R. Amey, Esq.
Aylesbury Vale District Council
Nora, Lady Barlow
Berkshire County Council
Bracknell District Council
Buckinghamshire County Council
Carnegie Trust
Cherwell District Council
Chiltern District Council
Countryside Commission
Crowthorne Parish Council
English Nature
Ernest Cook Trust
Mr M.B. Fellingham
Four Winds Trust
Friends of Vale of Aylesbury
John Paul Getty II KBE
Hammamelis Trust
Ms Molly Hyde
Inkpen Parish Council
Milton Keynes Development
    Corporation
National Heritage Memorial Fund
Newbury District Council

Oxfordshire County Council
Mrs Vera Paul OBE
Paul Ayres Memorial Trust
    (RSNC)
Pilgrim Trust
Plantlife (Timotei Meadow
    Project)
Mrs Joanna Robertson
Rothschild Executor & Trustee
    Company Ltd
St Helens Without Parish Council
Sandhurst Town Council
South Oxfordshire District
    Council
Trustees of Miss W. E. Lawrence
Vale of White Horse District
    Council
The Whitley Animal Protection
    Trust (through WWF-UK)
The Wildlife Trusts
Wilfred & Constance Cave
    Foundation
World Wide Fund for Nature

and many individual donors.

£2 off BBONT membership

If after reading this book you would like to become a member of BBONT simply fill in the coupon below and save £2 on membership.

Not only will you be helping wildlife – you will be helping yourself too:

★ **Free fold-out leaflet of BBONT's 20 main visitor reserves**
★ **Free local wildlife newsletter and diary of events three times a year**
★ **All reserves in this handbook to visit**
★ **Hundreds of organised walks, talks and excursions every year.**

HELP BBONT HELP WILDLIFE
Fill in the coupon today and save £2 on membership.

Send to: The Supporters Office, BBONT, 3 Church Cowley Road, Oxford, OX4 3JR.
Tel: 01865 775476 Fax: 01865 771301
I would like to become a member of BBONT.

BBONT membership rates (please tick box):
☐ Individual £16   ☐ Family £24
☐ Family and   ☐ Groups £30
   WATCH £30   (schools, clubs, etc.)
   (includes up to 4 children under 18)

I enclose a donation of £....
I enclose cheque/PO for a
total of £....
made payable to BBONT
or debit my VISA/ACCESS card no.

Expiry date ....
Signature ....

Name ....
Address ....
....
....
Postcode ....

£2 OFF BBONT MEMBERSHIP